JUST JANE
NX611

The Story of Two Farmers and a Lancaster

By Jenny Walton

ONCE THE GUARDIAN OF OUR SHORE
BOTH SHIELD AND ARROWHEAD OF WAR,
OUR SHINING SWORD, OUR TORCH OF FLAME,
OUR JEWEL IN THE CROWN OF FAME,
SHE REPRESENTS OUR ENGLISH PRIDE
AND BRAVE YOUNG MEN WHO NOBLY DIED,
SHE STANDS FOR COURAGE, FAITH AND WILL,
TO KEEP OUR STANDARDS FLYING STILL,
HER MIGHTY WINGS ARE SPREAD TO FLY
WITH GRACE ACROSS A PEACEFUL SKY,
GOD GRANT THAT SHE MAY END HER DAYS
IN SUNLIT CLOUDS AND TRANQUIL DAYS.

(Anon)

This book is published by Propagator Press, an imprint of:

AMS Educational
Woodside Trading Estate
Low Lane
Horsforth
Leeds LS18 6NY

ISBN 1-86029-800-1

Designed by Propagator Press.
Printed in Great Britain.

Cover picture 'Operation Lancaster' taken from an original oil painting By David Waller and published as a fine art print by Primetime Video Image C David Waller.

Images in this book taken from the videos 'Two Farmers and a Lancaster', 'Operation Lancaster' and 'Just Jane-NX611' Produced by Primetime Video, www.ptvideo.com.

This book is dedicated to the late Tom Walters, my dear dad, whose own experiences in, and love for, the RAF set me on the historical path I now so often tread.

ACKNOWLEDGEMENTS

My grateful thanks to all those who have helped me, in one way or another, research and put together this book:

- Fred and Harold Panton and their families.
- Primetime Video Productions.
- Flt Lt Mike Chatterton.
- Ian Hickling.
- (Last but not least) Mike Parsons for his patience, humour and invaluable help with editing this work.

FOREWORD

I shall never forget the first time I met *Just Jane*. It was Tuesday, 18 May 1993. At the time I was editor of *Lincolnshire Life* magazine and putting together a four-page supplement covering the 50th anniversary of the formation of 617 (Dambusters) Squadron.

To do this, I – and an independent photographer (who, with his wife, has since become a good friend of my husband and myself) – was given permission to accompany these World War Two veterans on their weeklong pilgrimage of reminiscences and celebrations. For me, that, in itself, was not only a pleasure, but also an honour, as I had read all about them whilst still a child – thanks to my father's library of RAF books. Meeting and mixing with these veterans and their families, day in and day out, for a whole week was a pleasure.

Part of their anniversary celebration was a trip to the Lincolnshire Aviation Heritage Centre with its Lancaster bomber, affectionately known as *Just Jane*. When we arrived, the aeroplane was stood outside the hangar, looking rather like a sleek, well-groomed living being, certainly not an inanimate machine.

I remember looking at her in awe, in wonder. Here was the very type of aircraft about which I had read so much as a child. Here, in close-up, was an aeroplane I had previously only seen from a distance at air shows,

It hit me - I was in love.

Or something like that.

Then, when Fred and Harold Panton allowed me over the threshold of and inside this wonderful aircraft, I could not believe what a difficult and cumbersome uphill route it was from doorway to cockpit, or, if you turned the other way – down to the tail end, where the rear gunner sat. It really brought it home to me that the tales of heroism about which I read so much all those years ago were really understated. It was no flight of fancy to feel, had the circumstances been as they were for those World War Two aircrews flying over enemy territory, rather as though I might be in a flying coffin. Yet it was obvious from the comments of the ex-Lancaster crewmen there that day that she was really representative of the aircraft they had all admired, one in which they had enjoyed a camaraderie that young men of today have been denied. They, too, loved *Just Jane*.

******

The next stage in my relationship with *Just Jane* came shortly afterwards when in the NAAFI with Fred and, over a cup of coffee, I heard the story of how and why he and Harold had come to acquire the aircraft, I then joined forces with

Primetime Video Productions to begin filming this amazing story. Primetime has now produced three video films, each one a continuation of the unfolding story as it happens, month by month, year by year.

Just Jane's story still continues.

I feel proud that I am involved in helping preserve her – both on film, and by means of this book.

It really is an honour to know *Just Jane*.

Thank you, Fred and Harold.

THE AVRO LANCASTER

Legendary aircraft of WWII

Designed by Roy Chadwick, built by A V Roe (Avro) and powered by Rolls Royce Merlin engines – the Avro Lancaster was the last and most successful heavy bomber of World War II. It is an aircraft remembered with great enthusiasm by its crews and has been variously described:

> "a young man's aeroplane…"

> "it had that extra speed…"

> "from a workhorse point of view, it was fantastic - their crews had

> confidence in them, and that was the main thing."

Between the years of 1941 – when the Lancaster entered RAF service - and 1945, some 7,377 of these amazing aircraft were built (four hundred and thirty of which were built in Canada). They flew more missions (156,192, including 116 under Coastal Command control) and dropped a greater tonnage of bombs (608,612) than all the other British heavy bombers combined. Few survived to make a hundred operational sorties and approximately 3,932 were lost during operations. Of the 47,000 Bomber Command aircrew killed on operations or missing in action, 21,750 were in Lancaster aircraft.

There are few of these magnificent aeroplanes left in the world today. Only sixteen examples currently exist in one piece, six of which – including *Just Jane* - are in good condition. Only two of these six remain in airworthy condition. One is Lancaster B Mark X, KB726, owned by the Canadian Warplane Heritage Museum, Hamilton, Ontario, Canada; the other being Lancaster B Mark 1, PA474, operated and maintained by the RAF Battle of Britain Memorial Flight (BBMF) based at RAF Coningsby in Lincolnshire – the *City of Lincoln.*

******

Situated not many miles away from the BBMF Lancaster there is, however, one other noteworthy and famous example of this magnificent aircraft…

CHAPTER I

Tail up and ready to go...

On a bleak, very cold day in February 2001 – the twenty-first of that month, to be exact – the public began to troop to the old, now disused, part of East Kirkby airfield in the centre of Lincolnshire. They had been arriving from as early as nine o'clock in the morning, via four wheels, two wheels and on foot, coming from all over the country to watch what was expected to be the greatest achievement of Lancaster NX611 since her operational days more than thirty years previous.

They were all there, wrapped up against the grey winter morning, to witness this aircraft – *Just Jane* – give a particularly special performance for her role as a Second World War Lancaster during the making of a BBC television film. Because this was to be such a momentous occasion, the film's director had agreed that some of her fans should be allowed to share it.

This would also be the first time in over fifty years that the somewhat aged runway, with its smattering growth of weeds and grass, would be accommodating a taxiing Lancaster. The fact *Just Jane* would be taxiing may not have been that much of a remarkable event in itself, perhaps, considering she had already displayed her mobility many times on the other side of the airfield where she is housed. The difference, today, would be that her pilot was to demonstrate she had reached yet another stage in her redevelopment: whilst taxiing, her tail would be lifted as though preparatory to take-off.

There had already been a rehearsal in private; now it was to be done for the cameras and her enthusiastic fans.

Everyone waited, as first one hour and then another ticked slowly by. The watchers could see plenty of activity from their positions behind a cordoned-off area. *Just Jane* stood, quiet and still in the distance, as people scurried around her. Occasionally, a tracking camera would roll past the crowds on its journey alongside the runway, carrying out dummy runs, ensuring all was ready before the actual filming began.

******

It was mid morning before her shivering fans; saw the object of their attention move for the first time that day. After a number of short runs forward and then back to her starting point, *Just Jane* finally headed for the main runway. The cold weather forgotten, everyone turned to watch, all talking stopped whilst cameras and camcorders were aimed. Amongst the audience were the farming brothers

Fred and Harold Panton, owners of NX611, their expressions alternatively etched with pride and anxiety. Although this aircraft, their pride and joy and the centrepiece of their Aviation Heritage Museum, was about to mark a new stage in her history, it would not be completely without risk. "Anything could go wrong," was the fear they constantly fought, each time her engines struck up and she moved.

Just Jane glided forward, steadily picking up speed, alone on the old runway. The sound of her Merlin engines, from being a distant roar, grew closer and closer, mighty and blood stirring in their power. Smoothly, she sailed proudly past the crowds watching from the edge of the airfield, gathering speed, followed by cameras both professional and amateur.

Suddenly, a collective sigh of pleasure and approval arose from everyone there – her tail had risen. She roared away into the distance, tail up, just a blink away from being airborne.

"Wow!" said a young boy.

"I wouldn't have missed it for the world," came from a middle-aged man.

"I started to fill up a bit," admitted a pensioner.

Men and women alike, child or adult, their admiration was plain to see. They settled back to watch *Just Jane* make several more high-speed passes, as the television company's cameras shot their film from every possible angle.

******

Just Jane's pilot, Mike Chatterton[1], who currently flies Nimrods from RAF Waddington, was once a pilot for the RAF Coningsby's Battle of Britain Memorial Flight Lancaster, *City of Lincoln* and was now a regular at *Just Jane*'s controls.

"Brilliant. It went as planned. I started off with a small amount of power," he explained later, "then let her trundle forward a short way before stopping her to make sure the engines responded and I could keep control. Then I increased the power – then more, and some more and, when we got to the stage where I thought there was enough, I made sure everything was OK and eased the tail up.

"A Lanc bomber hasn't done that on this airfield for more than fifty years," he said proudly, adding: "But we learnt during the practise run that you can't brake hard in a Lanc. Try it for more than three times and the brakes complain a bit. It was all very safe, though. Having allowed the brakes to cool off, I knew what power was needed to bring her tail up for about ten seconds or so for the film crew. Reminds me of my Coningsby days."

For a moment, his face took on a wistful look as he remembered his regular flights in that modern rarity – a fully operational, flying Lancaster.

"She's gone through a number of stages since she's been here at East Kirkby," he explained, referring to *Just Jane*. "First, getting the engines in working order again, taxiing, tighter taxiing, night taxiing and now – tail up. It brings that dream one step closer," he continued. "But it's a big decision for the Panton brothers – whether or not she should fly again."

He was voicing the thoughts of all who follow the fortunes of this Lancaster. This Lancaster had now been restored to such a high standard, it seemed only right that she should be given the opportunity to take o the air again.

******

So, why was she so important to Fred and Harold Panton? What was the connection between this aircraft and a couple of Lincolnshire farmers?

Just as with any good story, the answer has its roots in the past, in the days when Britain was at war…

CHAPTER II

The Pantons

Fred and Harold Panton are two of the eight children born to Edward and Frances Panton who were married in 1919. Lincolnshire folk, born and bred, Edward Stote Panton originated from Tathwell, near Louth, his wife, Frances Amy, had been born at Aby, near Alford.

Even as a lad, Fred's initial interest with flight was actually something of a disaster. He recounts a time when he was still a young lad.

"It happened in Spilsby just before war broke out, on Guy Fawkes eve," he says. "I had one of those Cannon fire-rockets - about three to four feet long, I'd saved for nearly a year to buy it. When my mother sold her sewing machine, she gave me a penny towards it."

Fred took his precious rocket outdoors, placing it in a jam jar, where it stood propped at a slant. He lit the touch paper.

" Mr Briggs, the fish and chip shop owner, was sat in his house reading a newspaper," Fred recalls. "When the rocket went off, it flew at an angle - straight through a small pane in the front window of Mr Briggs' house and right through his newspaper. It hit his ear before finishing up on a sideboard the other side of the room."

No doubt, today, Fred would have found himself up before the magistrates, but that was an era when people dealt with mischievous children in their own way.

Terrified at what he'd done, the scared young lad shot home and hid under the table, concealed by its voluminous grey cloth. Mr Briggs recovered his wits and went after the boy.

"I heard his footsteps coming. Then he knocked on our door. My father opened it and Mr Briggs said: 'I've brought your lad a stick to play with,' - and he handed over the rocket." Retribution came in the form of financial payment. "It cost me 1s 4d (about 7p) from my own money to pay for a new pane of glass. After that, every time he saw me, Mr Briggs would always say: 'There goes the Rocket Man', and he'd throw me a halfpenny!"

******

While his family of eight (Bessie, Evelyn, Roly, Chris, Gwen, Freda, Fred and Harold) were still young, Edward Panton took them from Lincolnshire where he had worked as a farm labourer, to the Osberton Estate in North Nottinghamshire, near Worksop. There, he was employed as a gamekeeper.

Fred and Harold clearly remember the bombing raids on Sheffield, which was only about sixteen or seventeen miles away from their home in the woods. During the blitz on the city, they saw dramatic night skies lit up by fires after bombing raids that sometimes went on from nine at night until six the next morning. It was all very exciting to the young teenagers, but their father prudently decided to build an air raid shelter for his family, hidden from the air by the woodland.

******

In 1942, the Panton family moved back to Lincolnshire, to Old Bolingbroke near Spilsby.

******

During those heady World War II days (1939 to 1945) of fighting for King and country, two of the elder Panton youngsters – Evelyn and Christopher – enlisted for the cause. Evelyn became a WAAF, and, in June 1942, Chris entered the RAF from the Royal Air Force Volunteer Reserve. He was enthusiastic about his new life; so different from that he had left behind in rural Lincolnshire. His first letter home cheerfully states:

> *...good food, and good beds, and perhaps more important, good comrades.*

Ever the conscientious son, he says:

> *I left the bike outside the booking office in the station yard[1] and they said it would be alright for a day or two but I would fetch it if I were you if you have not already done so. Do not worry about me...*

By the time he writes from his base at Weston Super Mare on 25 October, that same year, he proudly announces that he now weighs ten stone and nine pounds and is five feet seven inches tall.

> *...I enjoy life in the RAF, the food here is Excellent...how are Fred and Harold? I bet they are mischevous* [sic]

A few months later:

> *...I have just spent a pretty good Xmas. Thank you very much for the 10/-(50p) you sent me. I have been able to save a bit since I came here. I get £2.2.0 (£2. 10) per fortnight.*

Prudent, especially where money was concerned during those hard days, Chris wrote to his parents on another occasion from H Squadron, 4 Wing, Skegness:

...will you please look in the pockets of my clothes and see if I left a £1 note in them as I appear to have lost one...please send it along with my mouth organ...I am on the rocks until next pay day...I am billeted in the Windsor Hotel...I have a bed room of my own in which is a wash basin, hot and cold water and an electric light, so you will agree I am lucky.

******

Throughout his time on active service, Chris's letters are always cheerful and chatty. On 27 August 1943, he mentions having *been on 6 trips so far* including Turin, Peenemunde and Berlin. On 16 October 1943, he wrote from c/o Sergeants Mess, 419 Squadron RCAF, Middleton St George in County Durham. Referring to a young woman with whom his parents knew he had been friendly, he jokingly told his family:

I changed my mind at the last minute about marrying this girl and guess I don't care for her after all. She has got bad teeth.

Perhaps that reminded him to continue thus:

I would appreciate a couple of apples or so if you could get me some...

No doubt his being part of a Royal Canadian Air Force squadron had influenced Chris's communication skills, as can be seen by the use of "I guess" in the above letter. In the same letter, ever cheerful with his lot, he also gave his family the following description of a return from one of the squadron's sorties:

...After coming back from the last Hanover raid we were diverted (due to weather conditions) and so we put down at a Fortress station in Norfolk. We spent 3 days there and did we have a good time. We lived like kings as far as food was concerned. Tinned fruits – pears, peaches etc after each meal...

The next month, November 1943, he wrote to his sister, Bess, asking what she would like for Christmas, stating that, for himself, he would *very much like a fountain pen if you can possible get hold of one.* Then immediately back to practical matters – that is, food - he asks,

Has Dad killed the pig yet. Hope they save me some. I am looking forward to a big slice of Hot roast with Apple sauce.

That same month he sent another letter to his parents in which he explained when he had finished his training for *these new Halifax...The kites here are a new kind of being, a Radial-engined Halifax,* he would be home in perhaps three or four weeks time.

Almost all of Chris's letters home make mention of his father *getting hold of many rabbits,* an important necessity in those times of strict rationing, both for home use and for sale, and an activity which he obviously enjoyed and in which he had regularly partaken - both before joining up and during each leave.

> *...I hope you are keeping well & that there are plenty of rabbits for me to shoot...have you started harvesting yet?...*

His letter dated 5 January 1944 continues the rabbit theme and includes another example of his humour where ladies are concerned:

> *...sorry to hear you have not been having such good catches lately as far as rabbits are concerned. Glad to hear Bessie has found me a pen...Incidently [sic] I changed my mind and did not get married after all.*

******

Evelyn's letters home are chatty, too, although she openly states she does not enjoy active service anything like as much as Chris. Writing from the officers' mess, mostly at a Rudloe Manor², near Box in Wiltshire, she once confirmed this by saying:

> *...Glad to hear Chris is OK enjoying life he does take an interest in the RAF, different to me...*

One letter tells her parents she has located a watch for Chris, at a cost of £5. 10s (£5. 50). She asks that the money be forwarded from them to her by registered post. Evelyn always remembers her younger brothers, too, carefully placing Xs within her messages, *...for Harold and Fred.*

******

On 6 February 1944, Chris happily talks of his expected and imminent long awaited leave to come home. He also describes his fellow crewmembers – *1 Yank and 5 Canadians, all very nice chaps. I am the youngest in our crew.*

Along with Chris, the flight engineer, there was Pilot Officer Christian Nielsen from New York, of Danish Ancestry and known as "the mad Dane"; W/O2 Leo Milward, bombardier; W/O2 Don Awrey, navigator; W/O1 H G "Harry" Cooper, wireless operator; and W/O2 J G McLaughlin ("Moe") the Rear Gunner; and Air Gunner Sgt J S Thompson.

******

A later letter states...*only 6 more operations to carry out and I am through, having paid a visit to Stuttgart the other night...*followed by the proud announcement that he should be receiving his commission – from Flight Sergeant to Pilot Officer - any day.

Twenty-three days later came the news:

Today I spent 3 hours flying at 24,000 feet with the temperature 45° C below zero...first time I have been so high in daylight...I have now over 350 flying hours to my credit and I have the highest number of ops in my station to my credit. I have now only nine more to do...I will be home onleave the sixth of March...I hope Evelyn will be able to get [home on leave, also].

On 23 March, Chris wrote home, optimistically saying *...only five more ops...*

Strangely, this letter ended somewhat differently – instead of the usual closing with "from your son Chris" he closed with *from Chris* and added nine crosses, each denoting *a* kiss – one for each member of his family back home, maybe?

It was the last letter the Panton family received from him.

Meanwhile, in ignorance of the fact his son would never receive it, Edward Panton wrote to his son from his home in Old Bolingroke, addressing him as *Dear Son Chrissie* and informing him he had suffered from bronchitis. It was the 27 March 1944.

But, at just nineteen years of age, Christopher Whitton Panton, a young man who enjoyed life to the full, and who never burdened his loved ones about the extreme fear and stress he and his fellow RAF bomber crews must have suffered time and time again, had been killed.

CHAPTER III

The Nuremburg Raid

Chris Panton had been flying in one of the 214 Halifax bombers that left England on the night of 30th/31st March 1944. At that time, he and his fellow crewmembers were part of 433 Squadron, based at RAF Skipton-on-Swale, near Thirsk in North Yorkshire. Before leaving, he had proudly tucked away in his locker a letter confirming the news received earlier of his promotion to Pilot Officer, with effect from 2 March. His service number had also changed, from 1686348 to 175557.

Chris and the rest of the crew were part of a force that also included 572 Lancaster bombers and nine Mosquitoes, all having been dispatched to bomb Nuremburg in Germany. The Halifax in which Chris was flying, 111 BM'N', Code HX 272, unusually carried eight men, the extra being a pilot in training - Flight Sergeant W F Rost. Time of take-off was recorded as 21.49 hours.

That night there was a full moon. It should have been a stand-down period, but the raid had been planned on the basis of an earlier forecast indicating protective high cloud on the outward journey, but with the target area clear for ground-marked bombing. Despite a report from a meteorological reconnaissance Mosquito, which returned with the information that the situation was actually the opposite of that desired – that is, the only cloud present was over the target area – the powers-that-be decided the proposed raid should still be carried out.

Regardless of any personal doubts they may have had about the wisdom of such a mission in adverse conditions, the crews were obliged to obey their orders. The result was a disaster.

******

Ignoring all diversions, the German night-fighters had assembled along the two radio beams flanking the route to Nuremburg, the first of which took their place just before the British-based bombers approached the Belgian border. A furious hour-long battle ensued – lit up by merciless moonlight.

Eighty-two allied bombers were lost even before they had reached their goal, while many others lost their positions in the bomber stream through having to take violent evasive action, thus greatly reducing the concentration of the attack.

In the ensuing disarray and as a result of badly forecast winds creating navigational problems, a couple of pathfinder aircraft dropped markers at Schweinfurt, fifty miles northwest of the target. The result was that a number of aircraft – the figure is believed to be one hundred and twenty - dropped their bombs on the wrong target. Unable to see due to heavy dark cloud over the target areas, and hampered by strong crosswinds, other pathfinders also marked too far to the east of Nuremburg.

Although most of the crews initially believed they had hit Nuremburg, the town itself actually suffered little damage, with a loss of only sixty-nine lives – a comparatively small number that would have been far higher had the raid been successful.

Under heavy attack by enemy night-fighters throughout the raid, many of the remaining Pathfinder and Main Force aircraft also fell from the skies. Bomber Command lost ninety-five (ninety-six according to Martin Middlebrook) aircraft that night – it's heaviest single-raid loss of the war.

Chris was one of the 665 aircrew, who never returned. He had been flying his twenty-seventh major (with 6 Gardening) operational flight over enemy territory - thirteen with 419 (Moose) squadron, Middleton St George, and fourteen with 433 (Porcupine) Squadron. The Halifax in which he was flying was at 21,000 feet, nearing the target, when it was fired upon by an enemy night fighter. It crashed at Friessen, six and a quarter miles southeast of Bamburg, with the loss of five of its crew's lives. The surviving three were taken prisoner.

As Captain Ron Mundy, ex-57 Squadron, who also took part in the debacle, was to say in a film interview[1] many years later, "It was one of those nights when we expected the raid to be cancelled. The met forecast was not up to its earlier promise; aircraft were dogged by condensation trails for any nightfighters to take advantage of among the bomber stream. They were like foxes in a henhouse. The carnage was quite incredible..."

He explained, "The aircraft in the earlier sequence of the raid, namely the pathfinders and backers-up (57 Squadron were backers-up that night), were not unduly damaged. It was the later waves that came up from the rear because there was a twenty-minute stream of aircraft onto these targets, and the people in the last half did suffer quite badly.

"...ninety-five aircraft were lost due to enemy action and crashes, and two more collided at some stage of the operation."

Ron Mundy remembers looking back, as they turned and headed for home. "The track looking back down from the Nuremburg area was clearly marked out by aircraft burning."

One of Chris's surviving crewmates, Harry Cooper, says[2], "We were surprised, even at the briefing, of the route and the weather. It was a clear night and it was a long trip and the general opinion was we didn't like it."

Shaking his head, he continued, "We were early and the winds were a little stronger than predicted so, just before our rundown into Nuremburg we went out on a dogleg to use up time, because you want to get as many of you over the target at the same time as you can for protection...We were just turning onto course and the second dickie[3] landed over beside me. I went over to see what was the matter with him and I got on the intercom and the skipper said, 'Get ready to bail out', and then I could see the flame.

"That was it. I got over to the escape hatch. The bomb-aimer was there, and the navigator was half way out – and [then] she blew up…"

******

At first, Mr and Mrs Panton were told that Chris was "missing". The RCAF kept in touch with them at their home, now The Mill Cottages, Partney, near Spilsby, to which they had recently moved. Each letter, however, confirmed there was still no news of Chris or the rest of his crew:

> *No one at the Squadron had any contact with your son's crew after take-off and nothing that could be connected with them was known by the crews that returned. However, no news can be very good news…* (18 April 1944)

******

During this long and anxious time of no news, Evelyn's letters home always contained a note of optimism – "missing" meant he would be *back again sooner than we expect."*

CHAPTER IV

We'll always remember Chris

Official notification came on the 4 January 1945, that Chris was presumed dead. But the family, unwilling to accept Chris was lost to them, kept alive their hopes for his well being. On 1 May 1945, the International Red Cross replied to a letter they had received from Mrs Panton, explaining it was impossible to give her *any precise indication of how long it takes for names of prisoners of war to come through from the organisation at Geneva.*

The Air Ministry at Oxford Street in London wrote to the Pantons on 23 May informing them that a report had been received from the International Red Cross Committee stating that PO Nielsen, W/O1 H Cooper and W/O2 J G McLaughlin were prisoners of war in Germany. It also confirmed the fact the other five crew, including Chris, were dead.

> *He lies with his Air Gunner, Sgt J S Thompson, in a comrades graves, Numbers 4 and 5, in the cemetery at Buttenheim about twenty-three miles north of Nuremberg. The other 3 crew members are in adjoining graves…*(4 January 1945)

The site for this war cemetery had been carefully chosen, the letter continued, because of its natural beauty and peaceful surroundings. The graves would be tended in perpetuity by the British staff of the Imperial War Graves Commission.

> *…The loss of one of our most experienced and efficient crews under the captaincy of P/O Nielsen, this being their 27th trip, is keenly felt by the remainder of the Squadron.*

(As written by W/C C B Sinton, Officer Commanding No 433 (RCAF) Squadron)

******

Nearly five months later, Mrs Panton received a touching and emotive letter from one of the survivors, F/O McLaughlin:

> *You will probably want to know what happened to us on that fateful night…we were about to run up on the target and all of a sudden a flame swept past my rear turret. Chris reported to the Skipper "Starboard engine on fire, Skipper." The Pilot tried unsuccessfully to extinguish the flames but to no avail. The Plane then went in an uncontrollable dive in which Nielsen could do nothing. He then told the crew to "abandon aircraft fast". I did not waste any time, but I went through the turret…Chris Nielsen and Harry Cooper were blown through the side of*

the aircraft when it exploded at about 15,000ft or so. It was a fluke. They owe their lives I believe to the Lord. What I cannot understand is if the Lord helped Chris [Neilsen] and Harry! why didn't I get killed & let Chris escape unscathed. If anyone had a right to live it was this Panton! Gladly would I have laid my life down for Chris. He was the truest friend I have ever had…We were not allowed to attend the funeral & it broke my heart.

At the time I went missing…I owed him a pound note. So I enclosed a postal order for the sum.

Chris was always talking about his mother, father & his wee brothers who used to shoot with him when he was on leave. He certainly did love you Mrs Panton and I would be proud of him. He gave his life to protect people like ourselves. I owe Chris more than I can ever repay. He was the kind of a boy I wish I could have been. Chris was my Pal!

…It was a pleasure to know such a gallant, brave chap as Chris. If I can ever do anything for you I will be only too pleased.

The Pantons also had a visit from pilot Chris Nielsen, bringing his condolences and memories of the times he and Chris and the rest of the crew shared together.

******

"I was only thirteen when Chris was killed," Fred recalls. "I remember that time very vividly."

Harold was ten and a half. "I remember Chris used to like Palm toffee," he says. "He was very fun-loving, high spirited and he would always stand up for himself. He liked ferreting and pigeon shooting.

"After he joined up, we didn't see so much of him."

******

Amongst other letters that have been kept by the Panton family is one from a Margaret Laming, mother of Roger, who was a friend of Chris when they were lads. Younger than Chris, Roger died when he was almost fourteen – of what cause, we do not know. Mrs Laming wrote to Chris's mother:

You will no doubt be surprised to receive a letter from me as we have never met; but as I knew your boy Chris so well, I felt I must write to you…they were boy scouts, and got on so well together…I thought you might like to hear this little incident which I overheard one night…Roger asked Chris "Do you say your prayers at night, Chris?" and the reply in rather a shy sort of way was "Well yes I always pray for my little sister"

[Freda] *so he must have been very fond of her...only Mothers know the heartaches of other Mothers who have been through the same experience.*

******

In 1949, Edward Panton moved his family to a smallholding, Lowfield Farm, near Stickford, which he had purchased.

CHAPTER V

A Tiger Force Orphan

Meanwhile, the war continued its merciless destruction of lives and lands. The primary aim - right from the Second World War's early days - was victory in Europe, followed by the defeat of Japan. As 1944 came to a close, the former was assured; so plans for the latter were put into effect.

To this end, Bomber Command was designated for a special task.

On 20 October 1944, the proposal for an unusually large bomber force was implemented. Code-named *Tiger Force*, it consisted of thirty Lancaster squadrons, armed and trained to carry out a strategic heavy bombing offensive against mainland Japan, from bases in Eastern India and Okinawa. The operation was due to begin on 15 August 1945.

This *Tiger Force* comprised three Very Long Range (VLR) bomber groups, each made up of twenty-two bomber, fighter and transport squadrons - one RAF, one RCAF (based upon 6 Group), and one a composite of RAF, RAAF, RNZAF and SAAF squadrons. *Tiger Force*'s RCAF squadrons were converted to the Canadian built Lancaster Mk X bombers, which they flew back to RCAF stations in Nova Scotia - Debert, Greenwood, Dartmouth and Yarmouth - for training and reorganisation.

Later the bomber strength of the *Tiger Force* groups was reduced from twelve squadrons to ten and finally to eight and, by spring 1945, there were just two groups left, with the Avro Lancaster forming the backbone of the force.

******

The aircraft that was eventually to become known as *Just Jane* had been built at Longbridge near Birmingham by Austin Motors, in April 1945, part of one of the third production batch of a hundred and fifty B Mk VII Avro Lancasters (Contract Number 2827) destined to be part of the RAF's *Tiger Force* operation.

Given the registration NX611, she was fitted with a Martin dorsal turret and a Frazer Nash FN 82 rear turret, both equipped with two 0.5-inch guns; her front turret carried two Browning .303 machine guns. Her four Rolls Royce Merlin 24 engines, each of 1640 horse power driving three-bladed Hamilton constant speed Hydromatic propellers, were especially suitable for operations in the tropics.

With a maximum all up weight of 72,000 pounds (32,660 kg), a maximum landing weight of 60,000 pounds (27216 kg) and the ability to carry a maximum bomb load of 18,000 pounds (8165 kg) this Lancaster was a powerful machine. She had a span of one hundred and two feet; her length was sixty-nine feet and eleven inches, height twenty feet six inches, and her wing area was one thousand, three hundred square feet.

All in all, she was a magnificent machine that could have been cumbersome and unwieldy to handle. But, with a maximum speed of two hundred and seventy-five miles per hour at 15,000 feet, a cruising speed of two hundred miles per hour (at the same height) and a service ceiling of 25,000 feet, she was perfectly capable of keeping her crew out of trouble against enemy fire. Whilst carrying a full bomb load, her take-off run was around 4,000 feet, with a rate of climb of two hundred and fifty feet a minute, and the range over which she could carry that bomb load was 2,350 miles. In times of trouble, her pilot knew her stalling speed would be ninety-two miles per hour with flaps and undercarriage down at 50,000 pounds (26,800 kg) weight.

Some of the comments heard many decades later by surviving ex-Lancaster crewmembers illustrate their love and respect for the aircraft that carried them to and from so many operations:

♦ "It was the amount of punishment they could survive. On one occasion, we were going into Berlin…we were attacked by a nightfighter as we went into the target and I overreacted with evasive action and we performed what is known as a highspeed stall. The aeroplane flipped over onto its back…with about 12,000 pounds of bombs on board…By dint of God's help and good luck we rolled it out and although we lost ten thousand feet of height, we came back on an even keel again. It survived that. No aeroplane, today, could. Even your Tornados would be a bit hard pushed to do that sort of thing!" *Captain Ron Mundy, ex-57 Squadron)*[1]

♦ "Queen of the skies…a great aeroplane. I owe my life to it…*Jack Curry DFC*

♦ It had that extra speed…from the warhorse point of view, it was fantastic…the crews that went flying in them had confidence in them, and that was the main thing. *Bert Dowty, Air gunner, ex-44 Squadron*[1]

♦ We were on a raid in April 1943…just before we got to the target another aircraft had a direct hit and blew up. We couldn't see very much because we were in cloud and it [the explosion] just threw my aeroplane about the sky. We did one and a half loops before I could retain normal control…and the unfortunate thing was I still had a full bomb load on…we got there and back safely. *Squadron Leader William (Pil) Pilgrim, ex-44 Squadron*[1]

✳✳✳✳✳✳

But international conflict was nearing an end. After Germany had surrendered on 8 May 1945, *Tiger Force* training began in earnest. Then, after atomic bombs had been dropped on Hiroshima (6 August 1945) and Nagasaki (9 August 1945), Japan finally surrendered on 14 August 1945.

Tiger Force was ordered to cease flying on 6 September 1945 and then disbanded.

******

Japan's early surrender meant the newly purpose-built Lancaster aircraft were suddenly surplus to requirements. Instead of seeing active service, they ended up in ignominious humble storage at the RAF Maintenance Unit, Llandow, just south of Bridgend in Glamorgan.

That is where *Just Jane* stayed until 1952, when, in April of that year she was one of a number of Lancasters sold to the French Government (reputedly for £50,000 each). The sale was implemented under a Western Union (WU) Agreement that decreed the French would help the RAF patrol the Atlantic and Mediterranean shipping lanes.

Painted midnight blue, with blue, white and red roundels superimposed with a black anchor, as was the fin-flash, she was converted to Maritime Reconnaissance standard. This included removal of the mid-upper turret, provision for ASV radar, and fitting of airborne lifeboat attachments. She retained her standard- style rudders; unlike the RAF's own Maritime Reconnaissance Lancasters that had Lincoln-type rudders. From her tail protruded a rear-facing camera mounting.

Bearing the code WU 15, she was flown to her new home from the Avro works at Woodford in Cheshire by a French Navy ferry crew on 30 May to carry out maritime patrol and air-sea rescue (ASR) duties for the French Naval Air Arm (L'Aeronavale), from bases such as Lann-Bihoue in Brittany, and Agadir and port-Lyautey in Morocco.

In 1962 she was given a major overhaul by the Union des Transports Aerians at Le Bourget, and received a more durable all-white colour scheme. By 3 November, she was on her way to a new base at Noumeau, New Caledonia – a French island situated a thousand miles east of Australia. Her pilot for the trip was Capitaine de Corvette Jean P Angelini, and her crew came from the Ferry Squadron, Escadrille² de Reception and Convoyage. Their route took them via Malta, Istanbul, Tehran, Karachi, New Delhi, Calcutta, Phnom-Penh, Singapore, Djakarta, Bali, Darwin and Townsville, finally reaching their destination after sixty hours flying time, twenty-three days later.

During their seven-day stop-off at Phnom-Penh, when the aircraft was given a fifty-hour inspection, the crew was instructed to fly to Seno (Laos) in order to pick up a cargo consisting of 10,000 rounds of ammunition – a five-ton load. Take off for the return journey to Phnom-Penh from nothing more than a five hundred-yard earth strip of runway bounded by tall trees, on a windless day and in temperatures of around thirty-four degrees centigrade, naturally proved to be somewhat worrying for all aboard the aircraft.

Operated by Escadrille de Servitude 9 S (Surveillance), WU 15 became one of a team of three Lancasters carrying out regular patrol, ASR, communications and liaison duties across a wide area of the Pacific.

During her time with the French, she was also sent on bombing raids over Indo-China.

However, after only two years, the three Lancasters were withdrawn from service, high maintenance costs and shortage of spares prohibiting their usefulness.

Meanwhile, back in the United Kingdom, the Historic Aircraft Preservation Society (HAPS), under the auspices of the group's chairman, M D N (Bill) Fisher, had been asking about the possibility of acquiring one of these Lancasters in order to ensure its preservation. Up until this time, though, they had had no luck. So it was with some surprise, and delight, that they received a letter from the French authorities in Paris. HAPS was being given the opportunity to own, completely free of charge, one of these machines, which would be flown to either New Zealand or Australia for them to pick up.

The Lancaster that arrived at Bankstown, near Sydney, New South Wales in August 1964 was WU 15. She was accepted on behalf of HAPS by Hawker de Havilland Australia Pty Limited (formerly known as the de Havilland Aircraft Company Pty Limited until the early 1960s, changing yet again to Hawker de Havilland Limited during the 1980s). Responsibilities undertaken by the company included the manufacture, repair and overhaul of civil and military aircraft.

But before she could be returned to Britain, WU 15 needed a thorough overhaul, followed by a test flight. That, and her flight home, would entail some serious costs – at least £10,000. Negotiations and fund raising began in earnest, with Bill Fisher working almost full time on the project, with the help of solicitor Bruce Miles who organised the trip from Australia. Financial aid was donated by; the Royal Australian Air Force, the RAF, the Hawker Siddeley Group, Shell Petroleum and Quantas (who loaned radio equipment for her flight back to the UK). Money was also raised from holidaymakers on Sydney's beaches and donations came in from historic aircraft fans all over the globe.

In April 1965, WU 15 underwent the necessary overhaul and test flight and, on 23 April, was finally repositioned to Mascot, near Sydney, in readiness for departure. The aircraft, still white in colour and bearing the roundels and badges of Escadrille de Servitude below her cockpit, then underwent a change of registration, to British civil: G-ASXX. A four hundred-gallon fuel tank was fitted in the bomb bay, supplementing her usual 2,154-gallon wing tank capacity, and two additional observation windows were installed in the rear fuselage, port side, and a standard Anti-Submarine Reconnaissance/Marine Reconnaissance modification.

At midday, two days later on ANZAC Day (25 April), the world's only airworthy Lancaster took off from the Mascot airfield on the first leg of her return flight to Britain.

CHAPTER VI

Flying Home

It took nineteen days in all to complete the 12,000-mile journey back to her homeland - seventy flying hours - landing at Biggin Hill in Kent on 13 May 1965. Her crew mostly comprised of serving or retired RAAF members and airline personnel, many of whom had served as Lancaster aircrew during the war.

John M Hampshire DFC[1], who captained her for the epic journey, was assisted by 1st Officer Douglas H Smedley DFC; 2nd Officer John B Nicholls DFC; Flight Engineer Don Delaney CMSA; Radio Operator Arthur Johnston; Navigator Keith McCarthy DFC, AFM; PRO Pat Kilvington[2]; Organiser and Flight Manager Bruce Miles; Flight Stewards George Parlby and Jack Birney; and Press Officer Derrill Farrer.

The initial leg of the journey lasted just two hours and fifty-five minutes, when she landed at Coolangatta, a trip that also served as an initial familiarisation flight for the crew. Once this part of the journey was completed to the captain's satisfaction, the tiring, lengthy remainder was accomplished safely. This included flying on to Amberely, then RAAF Darwin (where groundcrew stencilled the crew's names on the fuselage; then another ten hours to RAF Changi (Singapore) and on to RAF Butterworth in Malaya.

When she left Butterworth, she was accompanied by an RAF Victor and a Canberra aircraft, plus Sabres from the Royal Australian Air Force, for the first part of the trip to her next destination: Calcutta (Dum-Dum). Her following stops were Karachi, Bahrein (Muharraq), Akrotiri (Cyprus), Istres (Marseilles), until the final leg to Biggin Hill – a journey for not all of which the aircraft or its crew had the necessary papers of clearance. According to *Story of a Lanc'* (Brian Goulding, Mike Garbett and Squadron Leader John Partridge, RAF), her arrival at Akrotiri followed a nervous seven-hour dash *across the Middle East from Bahrein on rather doubtful diplomatic and route clearances. Over one country, the crew only just misinterpreted an order to land due to "slight radio difficulty.*

At every base where she landed, admirers flocked round – many of who were ex-World War II Lancaster crewmembers. For the whole trip, the engines had to be nursed very carefully; never the less, the alien looking Lancaster returned to England within seventy hours flying time, at four-fifteen in the afternoon, in perfect time to take part in an air display at Biggin Hill's annual Air Fair. During her final circuit of the airfield just before she landed, she was accompanied by a Shackleton Mark III.

Her final touch down was greeted by crowds of enthusiasts welcoming her back to her homeland.

******

Now having a grand total of 2,411 flying hours logged from new, the aircraft was promptly grounded by the Air Registration Board. The number of flying hours allowed for one engine and propeller had expired, so restoration work commenced. A wide variety of people volunteered to help, including, of course, members of the historical Aircraft Preservation Society. G-ASXX was stripped down to bare metal and all parts carefully examined and, where necessary, restored to the condition that would enable her to fly again.

It took the team almost two years to complete the work before her engines, propellers and systems could by re-certified (by engineers of Field Aircraft Services (Hunting Group).

Re-registered with her original RAF serial - the now well-known NX611 - it was1967 before the Lancaster was ready to fly again. Wearing a new coat of standard night bomber black and camouflage, typifying the Lancaster aircraft that flew out of Britain on their bombing raids more than twenty years previous, she now carried the code letters HA-P - a wartime Lancaster unit code (No 218, Gold Coast Squadron) as well as being the initials of her owners, the Historic Aircraft Preservation Society. She was also given the name *Guy Gibson,* at a special ceremony performed by that famous gentleman's father.

Her first trip after re-certification took place on 6 May 1967, but it was the following flight that was best remembered - on 7 May, the *No 2 engine failed to feather resulting in the engine over-speeding at 3200 rpm. The fire warning lights came on and the extinguisher had to be operated before the engine was cut. As if this was not enough, the No 3 generator went U/S, the intercom was dead and the port wing flap developed a two-inch droop in flight.* [3]

Forty minutes after take-off, the aircraft eventually landed safely back at Biggin Hill, on three engines, thanks to the skill of her pilot, Flight Lieutenant Neil Williams[4], an RAF test pilot and international aerobatic champion. There was further drama to follow, though, when she took her third air test, on 9 May. This time, complete hydraulic failure after take-off meant her flaps and wheels had to be blown down by the emergency air supply.

Finally, after a detailed examination by Field's and Hawker Siddeley engineers, a thirty-minute test flight was undertaken on 17 May. This was uneventful and she landed safely. NX611 was now on her best behaviour.

A couple of days later, on the weekend of the 19 and 20 May, she flew to RAF Scampton, near Lincoln, for the twenty-fourth anniversary celebration of the Dams raids undertaken by 617 Squadron, with a number of the original 'Dambuster' crews on board. When they reached Scampton, one member of the welcoming committee was none other than Sir Barnes Wallis, inventor of the 'bouncing bombs' used in the Dams raids, as well as the famous 'Tallboy' and 'Grand Slam' bombs carried by specially adapted Lancasters during the Second World War.

NX611's next trip was to appear in a display sponsored by the St John Ambulance Brigade at Blackbushe, on 2 and 3 September.

Neil Williams went on to captain NX611 on all the fourteen flights after her return to this country, ably supported each time by his navigator Flight Lieutenant Eric Hughes. Sadly, the number of public appearances were few, because of prohibitive costs – an estimated £2,000 to £3,000 per hour. One other display she attended was held at Filton on 15 June, but, by then, NX611 had lost her uniqueness - the RAF's own Lancaster, PA474, was once again airworthy.

PA474 gradually took over the Lancaster aircraft display appearances, as the Historical Aircraft Preservation Society members were unable to find enough sponsors to keep their Lancaster in the air. Eventually, the group ceased operating, handing its assets over to Reflectaire Limited which, in its turn, was given notice to leave Biggin Hill.

There was one job that had to be completed before the temporarily redundant Lancaster left, though. Her ailerons were removed and sent to the Hawker Siddeley factory at Woodford, and refurbished with new fabric.

CHAPTER VII

Grounded

On a grey, wet 30 March 1969, our Lancaster was flown to the former USAAF base at Lavenham in Suffolk where her codes HA-P were changed to GL-C, in honour of Group Captain Leonard Cheshire VC DSO DFC who visited the base. Although she never actually operated from Lavenham, she was maintained at the ready, thus giving Group Captain Cheshire the opportunity of taxiing her along a runway.

This site was only a temporary home. After a proposed agreement to lease the airfield turned out to be unsuccessful, our Lancaster left Lavenham the following year. It was 7 February, a wet and cold day when she headed for RAF Hullavington in Wiltshire – which would prove to be another interim home. On board the aircraft was a well-known face – actor Richard Todd, famous for his role as Guy Gibson in the 1953 film *The Dambusters*. During the course of the flight, he recorded a commentary for a television programme.

The aircraft was give a new coat of paint by two Reflectaire employees during her stay at Hullavington but, during an inspection by Rolls Royce and Hawker Siddeley (Woodford), a fault was found in her starboard inner engine. This engine was removed and taken, by road, to a specialist engine company on the south coast of England, where it was stripped down and fitted with a new cylinder head before undergoing a four-hour pressure test.

An X-ray of the Lancaster's airframe depicted only one fault – a small crack in an engine bearer – not a significant problem, however - so, after undercarriage retraction tests and engine runs, she was cleared on a special certificate of airworthiness for one three-hour flight.

That flight took place on 26 June 1970 when, at three in the afternoon, she took off from Hullavington for her very last flight – to Squires Gate Airport, at Blackpool. This time, she had a former 617 Squadron (Dambusters) bomb aimer, Ron Valentine, as a passenger. Sat in the Lancaster's nose, the place he had occupied during the war years, he was given a special, low-level, high-speed run over Lake Bala in North Wales, one of the lakes used by the original Dam Busters when practicing for the dams raid. The whole journey took one hour and twenty minutes and, apart from losing a couple of exhaust stubs while passing over North Wales, proved to be incident-free.

******

The idea was to assemble a variety of items and form an air museum at Squires Gate, with the Lancaster as the main attraction – hopefully still in flying condition. Although it was eventually shown this idea could not be realised, her engines were started up and she was filmed in February 1971, taxiing for ITV's *Family at War* series. Later that same year, October, her guns[1] – considered a security risk - were removed by Ken Hillman, an armament specialist from the British Aircraft Corporation's factory at nearby Warton.

During her first summer at Blackpool, the Lancaster bomber was the subject of much interest, with crowds flocking in their thousands to see her. For a small charge, many of them were allowed to enter and look around inside the aircraft. Other items on display at the museum were a Seafire, a Sabre jet fighter, a Mew Gull and several wartime military vehicles.

Sadly, lack of adequate revenue meant the museum project became financially non-viable. The company was liquidated and everything made ready to go under the hammer of Mr Rupert Spencer, from Henry Spencer and Sons of Retford, Nottinghamshire, in April 1972.

The Lancaster was advertised as one of the lots for auction.

The *City of Lincoln*, flies overhead in greeting. *(Author's collection)*.

Just Jane, sets off on another taxi run, to the delight of all present. (*Author's collection*).

Just Jane returns to the hangar after another successful taxi run. The Hispano Suiza 20mm cannon is a typical 'local air defence' weapon of the WW2 period. (*Author's collection*).

After another busy day, *Just Jane* turns for home, to be returned to the hangar. (*Author's collection*).

Setting off down the runway and ready for the cameras. *(Primetime Video Productions).*

Tail-up and just itching to be airbourne. *Just Jane* performs once more for the cameras. *(Primetime Video Productions).*

CHAPTER VIII

Laying ghosts to rest

Although the future of the aircraft was still unknown, her links with Bomber County were just about to be initiated by the brothers, Fred and Harold Panton who, at the time, were calmly getting on with their busy lives. They were both staunch Methodists, and Harold had become a lay preacher.

As adults, the brothers had matured into quietly spoken, seemingly laid-back but actually very shrewd, country gentlemen. Fred married Betty in 1956 and went on to have a son, Phillip, and then twins David and Jane; Harold and Lucy were married three years later and had two daughters, Frances and Linda, and a son, Paul.

The two men often thought of their elder brother, Chris. During the 1950s, Fred had begun expressing a wish to find out where Chris was buried. He and Harold also still wanted to find some way of commemorating their brother's memory.

One time, they heard of the forthcoming sale of a Halifax aircraft and thought they had found the answer. They decided they would like to buy and restore it, and maintain it as it had been during its working life during the war years.

But their father had a different view.

"He wouldn't hear of it," says Fred. "Dad told me he didn't want one of those things on his farm."

Edward Panton, still suffering keenly at the loss of his eldest boy, did not want a reminder of how his son had died. Mr Panton senior's adamant views also extended to Fred's frequently stated wish to go to Germany and visit Chris's grave.

"My father, he never wanted me to go. He wouldn't talk about it – didn't want to know any more about it."

Edward Panton had apparently blocked his mind to all aspects of Chris's death.

******

However, Fred and Harold were determined that, some day, they would do something to commemorate Chris's death and the deaths of all those who had served in Bomber Command during the 1940s.

******

It was in 1971 that Edward Panton – now retired, the family poultry and arable farm being run by Fred and Harold - did a surprising thing.

"He changed his mind. It was summer time – a lovely summer's night. I was going up to one of our poultry sites, Lowfields Poultry Farm, to have a look at some chickens," explains Fred.

He remembers his parents were sitting outside their little retirement bungalow on the poultry site, enjoying the evening sunlight, when they saw him riding past on his bicycle.

"Dad waved and shouted out: 'I want you. Can you come and see me a minute, Fred?'

"I told him I'd be there in five minutes; when I'd looked around the birds. I said I'd go back and see him then".

"Then, when I went, he said to me, 'Now what I want you to do, Fred, I want you to go to Germany and get me some photographs of Chris's grave".

I said, "I will. I've been wanting to do that for thirty years. I was amazed that he'd asked me, after all he'd said about not wanting me to go."

Fred set his plans in motion for the journey, intending to set off within a couple of months, when the poultry sites would be empty and the farm less busy. Meanwhile, the first thing he had to do was find out exactly where Chris was buried because, after the news had come through of the young airman's death, his father had not wanted to know anything, so great was his distress.

"I thought we were going to have to go to some records office – the Ministry of Defence, perhaps, to find out where he did crash."

But before Fred had the opportunity to begin his research, help appeared quite out of the blue. He was sat at home one evening reading a poultry magazine. He noticed a photograph of a poultry farmer called Martin Middlebrook, from Boston in south Lincolnshire who, according to the accompanying article, had written a book about the Somme and was now researching for another – about the Nuremburg Raid.

Even as Fred was digesting this information, a knock came at the door.

"It was a sales rep selling concentrates for poultry. He told me Mr Middlebrook used these concentrates – did I know him? I said I'd just been reading about him, in my poultry magazine."

Fate had set the wheels smoothly in motion for Fred's journey to find his brother's resting-place.

The sales rep asked if Fred would mind him telling Martin Middlebrook about Fred's need for information. The answer, of course, was affirmative and, to Fred's delight, he received a telephone call from the gentleman that very evening. It was arranged that Mr Middlebrook would visit Fred the next day – which he did, bringing with him all the information Fred needed – information that included details of exactly where Chris's Halifax had crashed to his present resting-place.

******

On Friday, 10 September 1971, Fred set off for a ten-day trip to Germany, armed with a camera and plenty of film, and accompanied by his friend, Derek Hipkin. Neither had travelled abroad before, nor could cither of them speak a second language. Harold remained behind to look after the farm where the lifting and grading of the potato crop was in full swing with the help of everyone, including Mr Panton Senior.

"We set off about ten o'clock in the morning, from Stickford, in a Renault 4L," says Fred as he smiles at the memory. "We had to get on the boat at Harwich, and it arrived at Ostend at half past nine that night. It was dark. We looked at all the lights of Ostend and I wondered, what have I set myself to do here? I felt very nervous."

Driving 'on the other side of the road' unsettled Fred initially, but he soon became accustomed to the change.

They took the auto route through Belgium and headed for the little village named Friessen, near Bamburg in Germany, relying on maps, road signs, and directions they had been given by a researcher of both the crash and grave sites.

"We never stopped. We drove all through the day, through all the villages, until we found a camping site near Friessen, at about three on Saturday afternoon. We pitched our tent and had a cup of tea. I could see the range of hills in the distance where Chris was supposed to have crashed. They were only about six miles away, northeast of Friessen. My friend wanted to call it a night, but I couldn't wait 'til daylight."

So the pair set off again. They drove around, scrutinising the landscape through which they travelled, hoping for a hint of where Chris's Halifax may have come down – a break in natural growth, maybe, or a patch where younger, post-war planted trees grew amongst the more mature covering a possible crash site. About two or three miles from the village, they saw some mature trees at the foot of a hill.

Then they saw a likely area – but to reach it meant crossing a field of about forty acres.

"We drove across it, without permission," says Fred. "We thought that if anyone saw us we could explain later."

They went as far as they could in the Renault and then walked up the wooded hillside. "It was limestone. After looking around, we were pretty sure it wasn't the place, but I took some photographs, just in case."

As they went back to the vehicle, Fred said, "You mark my words, Derek, we'll find somebody who speaks English before night is out."

Sure enough, as they reached the car, they noticed a man and a woman picking mushrooms in a large field nearby. They climbed in and drove across to the couple. Fred wound his window down and asked, "Can you speak English?"

"Just a little," said the man.

After explaining why they were in Germany, Fred asked if these good people could help. As she listened to his story, the man's wife grew serious. In a not too friendly tone, she told him that a Lancaster had crashed onto her home during the war, killing her father and mother.

"I didn't really know what to say to that. It took a bit of explaining." But Fred won them over and, once they understood his need to find out where his brother lay so that he could take photographs back to his father, the uncomfortable moment was over.

"The man started to write something on a piece of paper, but then he stopped and said, 'No, I'll take you.' He took us to the Burgomaster in Friessen, who was also his brother-in-law."

Once introduced, they were promised help and, to Fred's surprise, he learned that the Burgomaster had been a prisoner-of-war in Ripon, just five miles as the crow flies from Skipton - where Chris had begun his last flight only to end up at this village. Fate, it seemed, had played a gentle trick on the two men and their families.

The Burgomaster remembered the Halifax coming down, crashing on the side of one of the hills, spreading its wreckage for approximately six hundred metres. Some parts had even reached the village below.

The Englishmen were then introduced to the local publican who had lived in the village during the war. He remembered the occasion vividly, having found the pilot, Nielsen, in the churchyard. Harry Cooper, the wireless operator, had landed near the crash site, and the third survivor was found below the hills. They all three had been taken to the local dance hall and kept there until the police came the next morning to take them to Bamburg for interrogation.

******

Arrangements were made for Fred and Derek to meet up with their new friends on the Monday morning, when they would be taken to the top of the hill where most of the Halifax remains had been found.

This they duly did, riding upon a tractor on which a couple of extra seats had been fitted so that everyone could ride up the hillside.

The journey was about a mile long, and when they reached the site, Fred knew he would not have found it himself.

"They told us the Germans had had to make a way up there to get the wreckage down," Fred explains. "Then it was kept open and now there's a gliding school based there. Funny, really – to think that that's there just because of Chris's aircraft coming down."

His emotions were in turmoil as he stood there, thinking of his brother's last moments, of the deaths of Chris's fellow crewmembers and of the few who had survived. No one hurried him. He took some photographs and, finally feeling some kind of peace, went with them back down the hill.

******

The Englishmen's next stop was at the site where the broken Halifax's young crewmen had been first buried. Chris had been laid in temporary joint grave number, 11 G 4-5, in the local cemetery at Buttenheim.

From there, Fred and Derek travelled another thirty miles, to the other side of Munich and the war cemetery at Durnbach, where forty-eight men, including Chris, had been re-interred after the war.

Here, at the Dürnbach War Cemetery near the Austrian/German border, Chris's body had been placed in an individual grave, with a headstone. This picturesque site was the last resting-place for almost three thousand allied airmen.

It was the most poignant part of Fred's pilgrimage.

"You can just see the Austrian mountains from there," he reminisces. "When I saw Chris's stone and grave, it was a funny feeling, knowing his body was there. When I left, I walked more-or-less backwards so the last thing I saw was the stone. But it rekindled my interest in doing something special to remember him by."

******

Back home, the photographs were developed and four, including one of Chris's grave, were especially framed for his father. They were hung in pride of place in the living room.

Three weeks later, Edward Panton died.

His family then believed they understood why he had suddenly changed his mind and asked Fred to make the journey to Germany.

"It came out of the blue. It amazed me after all that time that he asked me to go. He must have known…"

CHAPTER IX

In search of a bomber

On the Monday morning after his return from Germany, Fred went to work, expecting everything to settle back in the old routine. This was not to be. Waiting for him was one of the poultry farm's employees, Madge Bailey. From her pocket she withdrew a newspaper cutting.

"You might be interested in this,' she said to Fred.

It was an advertisement for a forthcoming auction at Squires Gate, Blackpool, on 29 April 1972 – the next year. Lot number 63 was Lancaster aircraft NX611.

Harold remembers that day, one that was to change all their lives.

"Madge knew we wanted a bomber, she'd seen the models we kept in the farm office and knew our intentions."

******

At last the brothers believed their long cherished wish to set up a singular memorial for their brother Chris and all the other young men who died in action could, at last, be realised.

As soon as it was possible, Fred went to see the aircraft, accompanied by Madge's husband, Bill. He needed to know if it would be a worthwhile purchase, and what sort of condition it was in.

It was quite a long journey from one side of the country to the other, but it was a very excited Fred who made his way to the waiting Lancaster. Unknown to him, this journey was the first leg of what would prove to be a very long pilgrimage to acquire the memorial he had, by now, just about set his heart upon.

Together the two men drove from the east coast of Lincolnshire to Squires Gate in the Blackpool area on the west coast.

They found NX611 standing desolate, somewhat weather damaged and looking rather like an unwanted orphan, her fuselage partially repainted by the local ATC boys. Although she was not in too bad a condition, Fred knew, if he did manage to buy her, she would need a lot of money spending on her – both inside and out.

Yet it was a happy man who returned to Lincolnshire, now determined this was the aircraft for him and Harold.

******

Next, Fred needed to set in motion the means of purchasing the Lancaster.

His bank was happy to supply him with a letter of reference that could be handed over to the auctioneer as proof he would be good for any offer he might make. It was now just a matter of waiting for the auction, to see what would happen.

******

The big day arrived. Fred set off for Squires Gate in nervous anticipation.

When he saw the giant machine for the second time, she was standing lonely and forlorn but proud, amidst an interested chattering crowd of curious onlookers, as she waited for the bidding to begin. By the time her lot number came up, the crowd had grown considerably. Her engines were run, an impressive and stirring sound, but there were only a few hopefully placed bids. Most people just watched – curious to see one of the country's finest wartime bombers at close range.

But a disappointed crowd, and an even more disappointed Fred Panton, was not rewarded with a sale. No offer had reached the reserve price of Lot Number 63, so the lonely Lancaster was doomed to stay where she was – at least for the foreseeable future.

Fred returned home, sad and unsuccessful, his dream, just out of reach.

******

Eventually, the brothers heard that the Lancaster had been purchased by the Right Honourable Lord Lilford of Nateby, in Lancashire.

Eagerly, the brothers got in touch with him, explaining their interest and asking for first refusal should he ever decide to sell her on. This was agreed.

******

Lord Lilford had bought the aircraft with the intention of keeping her airborne. However, when he discovered her airworthiness license had expired, and that the cost of renovating her to the appropriate standard for a reissue of that certificate would prove to be very high indeed, he let her stand idle.

******

The months went by.

Looking forsaken and exposed to the elements, the Lancaster stood on the airfield at Squires Gate, slowly deteriorating. She had been moved near to the Airport Fire Section, where personnel kept a watchful eye on her, but, over time, considerable structural damage was caused, mainly by inclement weather. During a gale, the starboard wing's leading edge was blown back and badly strained. Aerials were broken; a window had been left open at some point, allowing wind, rain and snow to encroach into the cockpit area; there was also damage to the cockpit top escape hatch.

If someone did not step in soon to save her, she would be destined for the scrap yard.

******

It was about eighteen months after acquiring her that Lord Lilford issued instructions for NX611 to be put up for sale again. It would seem that the Pantons' patience was to be rewarded.

Fred put in an offer.

"I'd agreed a price with Mr Bracewell, Lord Lilford's agent," Fred says. "It was a concrete bid."

A deal was struck and accepted by both parties.

Delighted with an apparently successful conclusion to their long awaited ambition, Fred moved swiftly. He had to find a way of moving the Lancaster from its present site to East Kirkby.

Nothing daunted, Fred met this challenge by contacting the local Air Training Corps (ATC), of which his son, Phillip, was a member.

He spoke with Flight Lieutenant Watson, the ATC leader at Spilsby. Knowing Fred and only too aware of the farmer's honesty and good intent, Watson, a Second World War RAF veteran, agreed to try and help. He made contact with a Squadron Leader at Strubby, who was also keen to assist and who, in turn, contacted Squadron Leader[1] John Willis at RAF Scampton.

The timing was perfect. Unknown to Fred and Harold, Squadron Leader Willis' station commander had very recently called him into his office.

"He was still cross because they'd taken away his Lancaster to put in a museum, " explained Squadron Leader Willis many years later. "He said to me, 'John, I want another Lancaster. Go and find one.' I said, 'Yes, Sir,' – well, what else could I say! But I wondered what to do, how to fulfil this task."

It was whilst still puzzling how he might locate a replacement Gate Guardian Lancaster for RAF Scampton that the message reached him from RAF Strubby.

"I found out there was a Lincolnshire farmer, called Fred Panton, who wanted to buy one."

******

A meeting was arranged between the Squadron Leader and the brothers, the former curious as to just what these two farmers would be like. He went to Stickford and was very pleasantly surprised and pleased with the brothers' aims. A solution to both their problems could be sorted out, he explained.

They agreed that if the aircraft proved to be in reasonable condition, the RAF would dismantle and transport her to RAF Scampton, where she would act as the airfield's Gate Guardian for five years. Whilst there, RAF engineers would restore the condition of her fabric. After a five-year term of duty was over, she would then be brought, again by the RAF, to the brothers' property at East Kirkby, and reassembled.

This agreement meant that both the RAF and the Pantons would benefit.

******

It was then arranged that Fred and Squadron Leader Willis, accompanied by Squadron Leader Partridge, the latter an RAF engineer and also from Scampton, would travel to Squires Gate so that the officers could see the Lancaster for themselves.

******

John Willis takes up the story.

"When we got to Squires Gate, we found a very unhappy looking Lancaster with pots of paint in the back. She was sad; she was tattered."

Nevertheless, he was satisfied the aircraft was worth saving and, to Fred's delight, affirmed his suggested deal. It was time to set the 'acquiring a Lancaster' wheels in motion once again.

Fred contacted Lord Lilford's agent, Mr Bracewell, and the two men fixed a price. It was arranged that Fred would travel to the Lilford estate at Nateby with a cheque for the agreed amount.

But fate was due to step in and upset Fred's careful plans.

******

The day he went to Nateby with the money, Fred was accompanied by Squadron Leaders Willis and Partridge, and both dressed in civvies. They had gone along for the ride, at their own request, with the intention of staying in the background whilst the business was conducted.

"There's no need to say who we are," Fred was told. "We'll not come in with you."

******

It was a happy man who shook hands, later that day, with Lord Lilford's agent as they greeted each other. The business was proceeding smoothly, but just as Fred was about to hand over the cheque he was most disconcerted to be asked, "Who's that you've brought with you?"

Although he had been advised not to disclose the identity of his travelling companion, it was not in his nature – or religion - to lie. What else could he do but tell the truth?

The arrangement Fred had with the RAF was disclosed.

To his dismay, Fred heard, "If they'll do that for you, then they can do it for us."

A horrified Fred heard that the sale was off.

******

The journey back to Lincolnshire seemed long and bleak. Little was said as the three men travelled, disappointment all round. Fred sat quiet, still, deep in his own miserable and shocked thoughts. 'I've slipped up,' he thought.

When he had told his companions what had happened, Willis had immediately retorted, "That arrangement wasn't made with him. He's plenty of money. But we'll do it for you – your heart's in the right place."

Fred returned to Lincolnshire with his unhappy news.

******

Bracewell kept in touch with Fred, wanting to know if he had contacted Scampton to ask them about moving the aircraft.

"But I waited a week or two. Then I rang Scampton and said, 'You'll have to help him or he might let it go out of the country.'"

Fred persuaded the RAF to go along with Lord Lilford and his agent's wishes. Perhaps there would be another opportunity to buy the Lancaster. This was agreed in part.

"The Station Commander wrote and told me what they were going to do," says Fred. "The deal had to be renegotiated – they would move the aircraft away from Squires Gate to Scampton for Lord Lilford, but it would have to stand as Gate Guardian for ten years instead of the original agreed term of five years.

"He also told me I could have the privilege of seeing it anytime, that I could take Harold or a friend, go inside it. It broke my heart – I'd lost it for telling the truth."

******

On Thursday, 2 August 1973, NX611 was handed over to Group Captain R B Lockyer, Commanding Officer of RAF Scampton by Lord Lilford, and two days later dismantling began in readiness for the journey to RAF Scampton. By this time, there was little left in the way of Lancaster ground support equipment although some, suitable for adaptation, was borrowed from 71 MU Bicester. RAF Waddington also helped out, lending tools used to maintain PA474, the Battle of Britain Memorial Flight Lancaster.

As though lamenting her ignominious state as she was slowly and carefully stripped down, the weather remained bleak, wet and cold. One can only hope the sparrows whose nest was removed from the engine cowlings had finished with it.

******

The whole task took until spring the following year. The aircraft arrived at RAF Scampton in pieces. Her outboard engines and propellers were removed for lightness, and her main planes and tail plane for clearance when negotiating the airfield's main entrance off the A15 Lincoln-Scunthorpe road. The airfield's main gates and their metal pillars were removed to facilitate her entry from the road. Special reinforcing struts had also been constructed to support her tailwheel, which was left in place to improve manoeuvrability whilst she was being towed.

During April, she was reassembled at Scampton. Concrete and steel supports were constructed onto which the axles of her main undercarriage and tail wheel would be attached, allowing her to be secured in position. On 5 April she was lowered onto them. At last she was able to take up her position as RAF Scampton's Gate Guardian.

NX611 was officially handed over by Lord Lilford on 17 May 1974, at which time he unveiled a commemorative plaque and gave her servicing record (RAF Form 700) to Station Commander, Group Captain J B FitzPatrick.

Beneath the nose of the aircraft were displayed examples of each of the RAF's two largest wartime bombs. A 12,000-lb, (5445 kg) 'Tallboy' and a 22,000-lb (9982 kg) 'Grand Slam', the heaviest bomb ever dropped in action. Later, a trials version of the famous 'Bouncing Bomb', which was used by 617 Squadron, when based at RAF Scampton, from where they flew to attack and destroy the Rhur dams on the night of 16/17 May 1942.

All of these bombs were designed by Sir Barnes Wallis, who also designed the Wellington bomber and the highly successful R100 airship.

CHAPTER X

The airfield

Following the installation of NX611 as gate guardian at RAF Scampton, Fred Panton kept in touch with both Lord Lilford and the Scampton staff.

Meanwhile, in readiness for the day when they would eventually own an aircraft, whether it is NX611 or another, he and Harold began looking out for a suitable site on which to keep it. When land came up for sale in 1981 that included part of the disused East Kirkby airfield, which still had some buildings that included the World War Two control tower – although all in a bad state of disrepair, it seemed an appropriate location. They decided to purchase it.

******

East Kirkby airfield is situated at the foot of the wolds, on the edge of the Lincolnshire fenlands, and was one of the county's most southerly bomber bases. When construction work began on it in 1942, around eight hundred acres of agricultural land was requisitioned for the purpose and two minor roads were closed. It was built as a heavy bomber station of standard mid-war pattern, with the usual trio of paved runways – 4,800 yards (4,389 meters) in all - the main one running from east to west. There were three Type 2 (T2) hangars suitable for four engine heavy bombers, a watchtower and widely dispersed accommodation, amounting to some sixty ancillary buildings.

Its decoy station was at nearby Keal Cotes, Stickford, approximately seven miles further south.

Allocated to 5 Group, the airfield was open and ready for use by mid-1943, proving a great relief to RAF Scampton, which was one of Lincolnshire's main bomber bases, but was still operating Lancaster from a grass airfield.

Group Captain R T Taffe was the station's first commanding officer.

One of the Scampton squadrons – 57 - was moved to East Kirkby, whilst the other (617, also known as *The Dambusters*) was sent to Coningsby, not far from East Kirkby and also possessing concrete runways. This left RAF Scampton free for concrete runway construction. 57 Squadron (motto *Corpus non animum* – My body may change but not my spirit) stayed at RAF East Kirkby for the rest of the war, operating Lancasters.

On 15 November, that same year, 630 Squadron (motto *Nocturna mors* – Death by night) was formed from 57 Squadron's 'B' Flight and also equipped with Lancasters (code letters LE). This latter squadron also operated from RAF East Kirkby until the end of the war, being disbanded on 18 July 1945.

Along with many other airfields, East Kirkby had its share of German raids and self-induced mishaps. For example, on 17 April 1945, whilst Lancaster PB630 was being loaded up with two 1,000-pound (453.6 kg) medium-capacity bombs, the bombs exploded. This caused a chain reaction of explosions as a result of which three airmen were killed and fourteen injured; there were also civilian casualties.

The next morning, it was discovered that a total of six Lancasters had been written off and a further fourteen damaged. There was also severe damage to the airfield itself, causing operations to be temporarily cancelled.

On another occasion, Flying Officer E J Murray (RAAF), set off down the runway, bound for a bombing mission on Stuttgart. This was his first operation and he was taking off with a full bomb load – the only exercise that could not be practised during training. Another factor was that the runways were only just long enough for a fully loaded twenty-nine ton Lancaster to take off.

F/O Murray's aircraft swung to one side and, as it sped across the Stickford road, its undercarriage collapsed. The bombs exploded with a tremendous blast – breaking windows as far away as Skegness (fifteen miles).

Miraculously, there was one survivor. The rear gunner had been only slightly injured, his turret being one of the few parts of the aircraft found intact.

******

On 20 July 1945, Number 460 Squadron arrived from RAF Binbrook, as an element of Operation *Tiger Force*, although all training ceased on 17 August when that operation was cancelled.

During August, 57 Squadron was the first unit to be equipped with three of the new Avro Lincolns for Service trials, but for everyone at East Kirkby, the war was really over, although 460 Squadron continued with local flying. The Australians did 'Cook's Tours' to Berlin, and helped bring home troops from Bari, a seaport in Southern Italy, before being withdrawn from active service on 22 September 1945. They then held a farewell parade on 4 October, which was attended by Air Vice-Marshall Wrigley, before being officially disbanded on 10 October. By the 25 October, all squadron personnel had been posted to Gamston for repatriation.

In November 57 Squadron disbanded, reforming the next day at RAF Elsham Wolds.

East Kirkby airfield was closed to flying, although still retained by the Air Ministry until August 1947, when it was reactivated by a detachment from 139 Squadron, RAF Coningsby, who used it until February 1948. Then it was once again closed to flying and put on C & M (Care and Maintenance) basis.

******

During the 1950s, it was designated a reserve airfield for the USAF and its basic facilities were greatly improved. It finally closed in 1958, after it had been returned to the RAF and was held as an inactive site until April 1970.

Much of the old airfield had been given back to agriculture by the time Fred and Harold purchased their part of it. They used some of it to set up sheds for rearing chicks, but still held on to the belief they would one day bring the Lancaster there. Meanwhile, they also began to renovate what had been the operational part of the airfield. The most important building they had erected was a new hangar - an exact replica, and on the site, of the T2 type hangar that had stood there during the war years.

The brothers often took up the offer made by the RAF that they could visit NX611 any time they wished. The sight of her, stood like a mighty sentinel at the entrance to Scampton airfield was an imposing one. But, when he went inside the aircraft, Fred used to grieve that her condition was not as it should be. There was some maintenance of the aircraft by RAF engineers, but not enough was possible to keep her in pristine condition.

But all Fred knew was – he was determined to acquire this aircraft. As one RAF officer put it: "He hung on like a rat."

Fred concurs with that graphic statement: "There is no way I was going to let it go."

CHAPTER XI

"We have a Lancaster aircraft"

Time passed. The brothers built up their farming business. They waited, periodically taking time off to visit NX611 at Scampton. During her time there, she was given three complete repaints but, due to low budgets, her maintenance could not be as thorough as everyone would have preferred. Bob Nelson, Registrar of Bomber Command Association, said[1], "I can remember going in it when it was Gate Guardian at Scampton and rain was dripping in, there was algae on the windows. It's a different aircraft, now – been lovingly restored by dedicated volunteers."

******

In 1981, Fred, Harold and 'Moe' MacLaughlin, the rear gunner from Chris's Halifax, took a trip to Germany. They were away for a week.

"It was a moving experience to go to the crash site," says Harold. "I brought back a carrier bag full of bits. It really brought it home – how those crews had been through an experience together. It binds them. They think the world of one another; you can see that when they come here, to the museum.

"Some can't get over the main spar [inside the Lancaster] so well now, of course!"

******

In 1983, the Lancaster's ten-year tour of duty as the Scampton sentinel approached its end and Lord Lilford was ready to sell her. Interest in her future was shown by a number of different bodies.

But her price had altered yet again – it was now into six figures. Fred and Harold were faced with a very tough decision. Should they take the proverbial bull by the horns and make an offer? Lengthy discussions ensued between the brothers and their families. As Harold says, "There was a lot of heart searching."

"We had to get on with it, make our minds up," says Fred. "I knew if I missed it that time, I'd never get another chance."

He made another appointment with his bank manager.

"He had given me a reference without any problem when I was going to go to the auction at Squires Gate, but now, when he realised I was still after the Lancaster years later, he thought I was a bit crazy."

Fred remembers with a smile that occasion he went yet again to ask for backing. "When I said I was finally going to buy the aircraft he [the bank manager] thought I was losing my marbles. He said to me, 'I'll never get my directors to agree,' but I was clear as a bell in my mind. I knew what I was going to do.

"There wasn't a Barclays Bank in the country didn't know about this farmer wanting to buy a Lancaster."

******

Fred obtained his backing.

Then he contacted Bracewell and made an offer.

There was a lot of negotiating and hard bargaining.

"I'd gone as high as I could. Mr Bracewell told Lord Lilford that was as high as I could go. Lilford said, 'Let him have it.'"

By September 1983, Avro Lancaster NX611 was finally the property of the Pantons.

"I didn't know the RAF had also told Lilford he had to give me first refusal. I didn't know that until after I'd bought it", says Fred.

******

NX611 was to remain at Scampton for a further four years until, in July 1987; everything was ready for her to come to her new home.

Fred and Harold had had plans for her. She would be the focal point of a museum based on memorabilia from the 1940s, the whole a memorial to the servicemen and women who died for their country.

******

The RAF kept its part of the bargain.

The aircraft was dismantled, brought to East Kirkby airfield and reassembled. The task took thirteen weeks in all, from March until July 1987, and was carried out by eleven men from RAF Abingdon.

This was almost sixteen years since Fred had first seen her.

The establishing of Lancaster bomber NX611 at East Kirkby airfield was the start of the Lincolnshire Aviation Heritage Centre. As a museum, it opened in July 1988 and, at first, the hangar contained just the aircraft and a farm wagon - quite a different spectacle from today.

"We had bought that wagon for less than £2 from a man who lived at Partney, when we lived there," says Harold. He had farm wagons for sale and this one was a connection to our past. Then we started collecting more wagons until we had about thirty. We restored them, painted them."

The brothers also acquired a stagecoach and, using a team of Dutch Gelderlander horses from Leicester, Fred took lessons in four-in-hand driving.

But when the Lancaster arrived, they naturally became so involved with it that they had to make another decision. There was not enough time for both hobbies, so they decided to sell off most of the wagons and concentrate on the aircraft.

******

A survey made in 1990-revealed NX611 basically to be in excellent condition, both the airframe and engines appearing sound. Around her, the museum was gradually building up, in both the area it covered and the number of items on display. Other buildings began to come into use on the airfield, the NAAFI was opened for visitors to buy souvenirs and refreshments and, best of all, NX611 was attracting a lot of attention.

She was named *Just Jane* after the 1940s newspaper comic-strip character, and a depiction of that character was painted on her. This came about because; when Fred was in his teens he had seen the model, Christabel Leighten-Porter, the original Just Jane, at Skegness. He had decided there and then that if he ever had a daughter, he would name her Jane. This he eventually did, but, when NX611 was safely settled at East Kirkby, he decided another Jane in the family would not come amiss.

The fame of the two farmers who had bought a Lancaster grew. People flocked to the museum, officially called the Lincolnshire Aviation Heritage Centre, from all over the world. The aircraft, herself, was a delight to everyone who gazed up at her majestic being.

During the summer months, she was brought out onto the apron in front of her hangar, with the help of a David Brown[2] tractor, and many pairs of eyes moistened at the sight of her, especially those whose own memories of the war years were being reawakened. There is no doubt she was an awe-inspiring sight. Many who had never before seen inside a Lancaster aircraft were allowed through *Just Jane*'s doorway, amazed at the steep incline up to the cockpit area and the great difficulty there is passing through her from one station to the next – it involves ducking to avoid the roof, clambering over the main spar, and avoiding pieces of equipment and structure jutting out from the sides.

Then flows the wonder at those young men who had spent so much of their lives in such aircraft as this. Many were just boys by peacetime standards, facing possible death in the night each time they flew away through the skies above England and onwards over enemy controlled territory. When one is tempted to ask, "But how did they get out of the aircraft if it was hit?" the answer is, "They usually didn't." Not surprising when you consider the amount of flying gear they wore and the bulky equipment they had to carry on their persons at all times. The primary escape hatch was in the floor of the Bomb Aimer's compartment, and a further three hatches are located in the aircraft's roof, but all seem much too small to allow frightened, possibly injured, men a means of escape from a falling, burning tomb.

While her visitors' look, and wonder, *Just Jane* seems to look down on them with benevolence. Although she represents a time of much sadness and loss, she is also a reminder of an era when people learned to work together as efficient teams, looking out for each other and, more often than not, bonding for life.

******

One of the teams of people who played a vital part in the lives of the aircraft and their crews was that which worked in the control tower – or watch tower, as it was usually known by RAF personnel. That building was, and still is, the heart of any operational airfield, sited as it is nearest to the runway.

It has always been the focal point for aircrews, because it was where Flying Control was housed. It was where ground controllers talked to pilots before take off and landing, and where they were de-briefed after the flight. These control tower teams were the people who ensured airborne collisions were avoided, and who sent along the fire trucks and ambulances if something did go wrong.

The Aviation Heritage Centre's control tower is a two-storey building. Before the Panton brothers took over the airfield, it had fallen into ruin. They have completely renovated and refurbished it so that it now represents the original building on a typical 'ops' night. It has been said it is, in fact, one of the best depictions of a control tower in the whole country.

Each room on the two floors contains dioramic scenes of busy men and women carrying out their duties. Authentically dressed mannequins, surrounded by genuine 1940s artefacts, are displayed in realistic settings – amongst which are the pilots' briefing room, the duty pilots' and observers' rest rooms, the radio room and the Met Office.

On the first floor, the large Control Room, call sign 'Silksheen', has a constant background of radio transmissions between returning aircraft and the tower. It contains maps and various boards displaying such information as the crew roster, serviceability status, and battle order and target boards. This building has a powerful atmosphere that swiftly transports the onlooker back in time to those dramatic war years.

There is another, more ethereal tie with the past at East Kirkby and its control tower. Not surprising, this, that the airfield should have a ghost – most airfields are reputed to have one. But when you know that someone such as Fred Panton, an honest, unpretentious and practical character, is one of those who genuinely believe he has seen East Kirkby's ghost, then the idea of its existence is worth serious consideration.

It was a time when Fred was alone at the airfield after working most of the day and into the evening. He decided to take a ride to fetch himself some supper from the local fish and chip shop.

"I went in my Renault. I'd just got going. I looked through the hangar base towards the control tower and I saw this tall man walking towards the control tower and he looked to be carrying a big bundle of plastic bags. I stopped, because I'd not seen anyone all day, and I said to myself, 'Who the hanover's that?' I just thought, 'Don't suppose he's doing any harm,' and I carried on to fetch my fish and chips. I suddenly felt, when I got on the main road, that I'd heard about this before, and I thought, 'I bet that's the same man, the ghost, that I've been told about.

"I thought about it in bed, all next day, and I'm convinced that's what I saw."

The 'man' was dressed in USAAF gear. Perhaps he was one of the crew of a Flying Fortress that crashed nearby on 30 December 1944. They had taken off from an American base in Bedfordshire at nine that morning. The Americans used to fly their missions in daylight, aiming for precision targets, relying on extremely heavy defensive armament to fend off the German fighters. This particular aircraft, Flying Fortress number 29749, and its crew were returning from a bombing mission over the Rhineland.

Her pilot knew he would not make it back to base with two failing engines, so he headed for the nearest airfield in England. East Kirkby loomed ahead. It was an unfamiliar layout to him. The team in the control tower could see his approach was not right and signalled him to go round and try again. He was still not lined up correctly on the second approach and the aircraft was ordered to make a third try.

But the Flying Fortress 'ran out of sky' and crashed into a nearby field. There was an explosion; the fire was so intense it threw a huge black cloud into the unsympathetic sky.

Fred, who was thirteen at the time, was working in another field not far from the burning wreck. He saw the aircraft come down, ran to his bicycle and, jumping on it, made a speedy dash to the scene. He was there before the airfield's fire truck – not that it could make any impression on such a fierce conflagration. The little boy saw the burning fuselage and the shapes of the crew trapped inside.

Later, the bodies were removed from the aircraft, charred beyond recognition.

One can only wonder if it is one of those dead crewmen who now keeps making his way across to the control tower – for reasons we can only guess.

******

The control tower at Skipton-on-Swale, the airfield from where Chris Panton made his last fight, is a lonely ruin now, its runways almost lost beneath reclaimed agricultural land. It is also the venue of an annual pilgrimage. Every year, on the evening of 30 March, Fred travels there to stand, inside its shell, at the exact time that his brother Chris took off on his final mission in 1944.

Long deserted, but peaceful now, this control tower is the perfect setting for Fred to remember – to remember his brother and the last time his Halifax had rolled along the runway before taking off to leave Yorkshire, never to return.

CHAPTER XII

There's life in the old girl...

It had to happen.

The East Kirkby Lancaster quickly became established as an international attraction, the museum around it steadily expanded and visitors were flocking in their thousands to marvel and remember. Things could not stand still.

Fred and Harold decided it would be interesting if one of *Just Jane's* engines could be made to work again.

Of course, they were not the only ones to wonder this – more and more people were asking the same question. The aircraft was obviously in such good condition structurally, that it seemed right to move on another step and – as Harold says, "I particularly remember, one day, two or three gentlemen come through the door and say, 'She's made to fly...' We had to look at the possibilities. We decided to see if an engine could be made to run again."

******

That historic first move towards restoring one of her four Rolls Royce Merlin engines was made in December 1993, when the brothers decided to look for a suitable team to check out the situation.

Two ex-RAF engineers, Ian Hickling and Roy Jarmain, were brought in to do the job.

Ian first heard about the possibility of working on *Just Jane* one evening when in the pub.

"A friend of mine I used to work with when I was at RAF Coningsby, Mike Chatterton, came in. He said that Fred was actually thinking of getting an engine going – and it sort of progressed from there."

Mike Chatterton was, at that time, the pilot of the Battle of Britain Memorial Flight (BBMF) Lancaster, the *City of Lincoln*, by this time based at Coningsby. Ian, who had been serving as an engineer at RAF Coningsby, had joined the Battle of Britain flight in 1985, and gained invaluable experience whilst working on all the aircraft there, including the Lancaster (PA474). He had left the RAF in 1993, and, after a month of unemployment, went on to RAF Swinderby where "Roy was a team mate".

Roy, an airframe fitter, had joined the RAF when only fifteen years of age. He, too, had worked on and flew in Lancasters. "After I was made redundant, I went on to helicopters. I met Ian at Swinderby and he asked me if I'd assist him with this aircraft. Of course, I said, 'Yes!'"

Ian was keen to be the one to work on the brothers' Lancaster. He was sure that, keen after more than two decades silence, there was still a strong possibility it could be restored to full working condition.

******

The engine restoration project began on 10 January 1994, a grey, cold winter day, and the biggest problem they encountered was undoing all those nuts and bolts that had lain untouched since the 1970s.

"They'd inhibited the engine that well it was difficult to get a spanner on to take them off," explained Ian. "Once we'd got them all off, it would be just like a normal run-of-the-mill Merlin engine servicing."

Once assured the airframe was strong enough to withstand a running engine, the camshaft covers were removed, something else that had not been done since the 1970s when the last servicing was carried out. Upon examination, the camshafts were found to worn beyond limits and so were removed. Both were changed using replacements from the BBMF Lancaster stock – evoking memories of the days when, conversely, it used to be the BBMF's PA474 dipping into NX611's supplies.

The cylinder bores were in good condition, however.

Removal of the propeller was not a simple task, Ian and Roy not having the convenience of the correct equipment as used by the RAF. Using only ropes as slings, a forklift and plenty of careful manoeuvring, they carefully lifted it off, manoeuvred it manually, and transported it across the hangar to a waiting makeshift workbench. There, it was lowered ready for stripping down and examination.

Then the magnetos were removed, as were the fuel and coolant pumps. The propeller was stripped and, to everyone's delight, it was discovered that neither its base nor blades had cracked during transportation. It was then paint-stripped, examined and re-sprayed before being re-assembled – good as new.

After being stripped and examined, the starter motor, coolant and fuel pumps were sent for testing. Reconditioned and thoroughly tested, they were then refitted to the engine. All twenty-four spark plugs were cleaned and refitted, along with a replacement ignition harness. The radiator for the coolant was pressure tested to check for leaks, and found to be fully serviceable, and the oil tank was flushed out, ensuring it was freed from the muck that had settled in it over the years, making it again ready for mineral-based oil - the standard engine oil in use during the war years.

The replacement ignition harness was tested with a 'Megga' high-tension tester; the fuel pump was pressure tested and the fuel jettison system reset. The carburettors were removed, stripped, thoroughly cleaned, rebuilt, tested for fuel leaks and any other faults before being refitted to the engine which, itself, had to be flushed and oil-primed. When Roy uncovered the throttle controls between the cockpit lever and the engine, it was discovered that almost a third of the small control rods had corroded and needed to be replaced.

Any spare parts not available from normal sources were manufactured by Ian and Roy, themselves.

Local electrical contractors, John Butler and Peter Dixon, came in and completely replaced the electrical system wiring – which had all been cut when the aircraft was taken from Squires Gate to RAF Scampton under the assumption that it was never going to fly again. That alone, was a ten-day job.

When Ian was satisfied all was in order, they carefully replaced the propeller. The engine, itself, was left without its streamlined cowlings for the initial run.

Work on the engine was almost complete when the fuel arrived at the airfield – a donation of fifty gallons of 100 / 120 octane Avgas, (aviation grade petrol, usually known in the RAF as 'Green Goddess' due to the distinctive dye which was added to the fuel to prevent pilfering), and twenty-five gallons of aero engine oil.

Finally, everything was ready.

Whilst she was still in the hangar, her engine was manually turned, just to make sure it could. She would soon be ready for firing up.

Making their remarkable achievement sound simple, Roy explained: "It only took six weeks; there was very little wrong with it. Most of the stuff, like the magnetos, had already been serviced by the RAF while she was at Scampton."

After seven hundred and twenty-eight man-hours work from cockpit to engine, and at a cost of £7,000, number three engine was finally ready to perform for the public.

******

Before this, however, another special event was organised – a Memorial Service at the Aviation Heritage Centre to mark the fiftieth anniversary of the Nuremburg Raid. It was held inside the hangar with *Just Jane* as a living backdrop to the proceedings. Many special friends were invited, including John Willis, one of the prime organisers in getting the aircraft to her present home.

A serious occasion, obviously evoking much nostalgia and some sadness, it was attended by more than a hundred ex-RAF personnel and their families, as well as other members of the public. Wreaths were laid and the traditional two minute silence held, yet, once the service was over and the *Last Post* had resounded its final note around the great building, the gathering broke up with smiles, to talk, to remember and, of course, to admire the museum's own special token of remembrance – the Lancaster. She was later brought out of the hangar, to stir everyone's hearts as she stood in the open air - silent, yet proud, as though offering her own salute to both fallen and survivors alike.

******

It was a damp, cold evening on Wednesday, 20 April 1994 when *Just Jane* was eventually brought out of the hangar to try out her refurbished engine. If it fired up, this would be for the first time in twenty-two years. Another memorable factor was that it would also be the first time a Lancaster's Rolls Royce Merlin engine had been heard on East Kirkby Airfield in fifty years.

For insurance purposes, a fire tender stood close by – just in case…

With the its crew was Station Officer Hargreaves from Skegness Fire Station who was also acting as supervisory officer for other stations, including Spilsby Fire station – from where this tender had come. There at Fred's request, as "a standard precaution", he had to admit that it was "not often we get a request like this!"

"It's going to happen any time, now. I'm feeling a bit apprehensive…" Fred was heard to say as the old lady was brought out of the hangar. Once safely outside, with chocks in place, Ian climbed into the pilot's seat, looked out of the cockpit window and grinned. The small crowd on the sidelines added to the expectant atmosphere.

The old aircraft wheezed and groaned, coughed and spluttered, juddering with the effort of breathing life into this quarter of her power. The next few minutes were tense. There was an airlock to deal with before everyone heard, with relief, her 1600 horse power engine spit, vibrate slightly, and then - with more of a croak than a roar, the propeller began to turn. The engine groaned as it tried to keep turning, slowly and hesitantly at first, exuding a puff of smoke as inhibitor waste burned off. But with increasing confidence, it warmed to the task and then suddenly number three-engine burst into full life. Gaining confidence, the sound developed into a roar as though triumphantly declaring its pleasure at just being. The Rolls Royce Merlin held steady and, like a huge jungle cat, finally settled into a noisy purr of contentment.

The look of excitement and joy on Fred and Harold's faces, their wide grins of delight, spoke volumes. No surprise their eyes were moist as they looked at one another with wide smiles, then at their relieved families, before once again turning to gaze at their beloved Lancaster.

The rest of *Just Jane*'s small audience, immediate family and friends of the brothers, were able to release its held breath at long last. They gave a simultaneous sigh of relief and joy, turning to each other with grins, many unashamedly wiping at wet eyes.

Ian, a serious look on his face, listened to every nuance as the engine continued to turn steadily. When he deemed she had done enough for a first time, he began shutting down the engine. It slowed, stuttered as though in indignation, slowed some more, and then finally stopped. For long moments, an eerie hush covered the airfield.

Suddenly, appreciative applause rolled around the now silent aircraft; wide smiles showed delight and acclaim of this historic event.

Although speaking in typically quiet voices, Fred and Harold still managed to show their joy.

"I can't believe it now I've heard it," said Harold.

"Did you see that – beautiful," was all Fred could reply. "I was more emotional before it started than when it actually did. It'll be tonight, when I'm in bed. That's when it'll hit me."

Ian leaned out of the cockpit, his smile almost splitting his face in two.

"Music to the ears," was Roy's comment. "You just can't describe it – after working three months on it and it materialises."

Fred's wife, Betty, smiled as she admitted, "He's just been a little bit on edge...He's happy now. It's his dream come true – and that's what I wanted."

"Incredible for me! That is an achievement and a half," said Ian, after both his feet and his mind had come back down to earth. "To actually fire up that quickly after twenty-two years – I honestly didn't think it was going to go like that, not first time. That's the biggest achievement of my life. Just the two of us working on it – and then to just press the button and it started..."

There could be no doubt in anyone's mind that here was one very relieved as well as very happy engineer.

******

So, that was the practise run, maybe not as smooth as it once would have been, but a definite moral booster to the team to hear and see.

"We kept it quiet as much as we could," said Fred. "Didn't want too many, not first time – but a fair crowd came."

Obviously, as far as this particular 'lady' is concerned, there are no secrets; there is so much interest in what goes on in her life that news of anything happening is spread quickly.

The next evening, 21 April, the weather was a little kinder for the official start up to which the public had been invited, along with the media, so they could all witness for themselves *Just Jane*'s return to life.

That evening's audience, too, were delighted with seeing and hearing that engine start. Sounding a little more positive from the outset, and with just an initial whine of protest and a pop or two, the engine kept its propeller turning steadily before snarling and settling into a firm purr.

Afterwards, the engineers came in for plenty of praise from everyone, including Fred and Harold.

"To think it started up, just like that," was Fred's happy comment. "They had got everything absolutely spot on with the settings – or it wouldn't have started as quickly as it did."

Among the crowd were members of 44 Squadron who had watched the whole proceedings with critical eyes and ears. Comments afterwards were complementary and included such words as, "…a nice sound of those days when we flew in Lancs," and "It's an important piece of history, the Panton brothers have done a remarkable job with her."

CHAPTER XIII

The museum just keeps on expanding

Naturally, hearing the sound of a working Rolls Royce Merlin engine on East Kirkby airfield stimulated interest all over the world. Visitors were arriving in their thousands to the airfield at the edge of a little Lincolnshire village, eager to see, touch and hear this veteran who had been given her second wind.

The number of artefacts at the museum, within one or the other of the building around the airfield, continued to grow – items being donated by both individuals and organisation, creating a unique collection. One piece of shrapnel was brought in and handed over with the words, "This just missed me during the war. I picked it up and kept it." Small items filled showcases, larger ones floor space – in the hangar and in a number of other huts.

Letters, maps, newspaper clippings, telegrams, photographs, wireless transmitters are constantly being donated, whilst recovered aircraft pieces, each with its own personal and poignant story, and brought in by the Lincolnshire Aircraft Recovery Group that has its base at East Kirkby Airfield, hold fascination for young and old alike. So, too, do other rescued pieces of crashed aircraft - including a Vickers Wellington' wings, fuel tanks and side panel section; an Alvis Leonides 9-cylinder radial engine (520/540hp) as fitted to a Percival P56; a Provost training aircraft; and an engine Nacelle, still retaining its landing gear from a Wellington Mk1A, L7775.

There are parts of propellers from various aircraft, a Bristol Hercules sleeve valve radial engine, Rolls Royce Derwent jet engines and – to remind us why all this awesome machinery was developed in the first place - bomb racks and bomb shackles, complete with inert bombs, and a bomb trolley.

Grassy areas were landscaped, memorial trees to individuals or whole crews were being planted, dioramas appeared in huts depicting such scenes as a wartime living room, complete with letter behind the clock from a loved one in the services. All the furnishings that were found in 1940s homes are in situ, plus a radio broadcasting the latest information on the progress of the war, tape-protected windows, a Singer sewing machine (a commodity without which no self-respecting housewife could manage), and a black-leaded coal fire range with side-oven – over whose door socks are hanging to dry, and in front of which lies the inevitable home-made rag rug.

There's a wartime fire tender, an oil bowser, and a Queen Mary (an articulated lorry specially designed to transport large aircraft components such as wings, by road) which has been conscripted for carrying visitors on a three-mile trip around the whole airfield – an especially appreciated ride for ex-aircrews who have returned with their memories. There is even a David Brown tractor, as used for towing aircraft during the war years, which has joined the collection.

Another very appropriate addition to the Centre's memorabilia is an example of the bouncing bomb[1], which was found in the sea in Reculver Bay off the north Kent coast, at Southend on Sea.

"A gentleman came to the museum and said he knew where there was an original bouncing bomb, and although it had been submerged in the sea for all those years, it was in complete condition," says Fred. "It was too good to miss. The Lancaster and that bomb go together. I don't think we could find another one in such a good state."

The cost of purchasing and transporting the four-ton practise bomb from Southend came to just over £1,000.

The Aviation Heritage Centre was offering more and more to its visitors.

******

Just a few months after the successful restoration of the first engine, the second – number two engine - was successfully restored and fired up.

"We used exactly the same routine for this one as we did the first engine," Ian explained.

As the crowds thrilled to the sound of her two Merlins, they were thrilled to hear another four coming closer and closer – the BBMF *City of Lincoln* had flown over from RAF Coningsby to salute her sister aircraft on the ground. Three times she circled overhead, once coming so low that an RAF officer was hear to say, "I didn't see that!"

The pilot of the *City of Lincoln* was Mike Chatterton, then based at RAF Coningsby. Son of World War Two Lancaster pilot, the late John Chatterton[2], a local farmer who, naturally, was a regular visitor to the museum, Mike was flying over East Kirkby airfield – once agricultural land belonging to Hagnaby Grange and farmed by his father's family. The two men felt a tremendous affinity to the Panton brothers and their Lancaster, supporting them and the Aviation Heritage Centre wholeheartedly.

******

Once the thrill of hearing six Lancaster engines roaring out their greeting to each other had subsided somewhat, visitors went in search of refreshments from the NAAFI, or wandered around the airfield where they found the actual ground support vehicles used during the 1940s, including a Fordson WOTI/foamtender (*circa* 1941) amongst a selection of tractors from that era, along with bicycles, motor cars and trucks. They explored the brick-built underground blast shelter, an Anderson civil air raid shelter and saw a Bison mobile pillbox.

Inside the many airfield buildings a plethora of sights evoke awe and incredulity from the youngsters, but smiles of remembrance from their grandparents. A diorama gives an insight into the cockpit of a Heinkel He 111; there is an Anderson air raid shelter depicting only too clearly the cramped, dark conditions endured by those who were forced to seek its protection; a display of mementoes from the USAAF's time in Lincolnshire; a large display case containing model aircraft of every description, and another diorama depicting WAAFs at work on radio repairs. British and German uniforms, original photographs of bomb damage to Cologne, Hamm, Essen and Bremen, and photographs from when a German incendiary bomb dropped on Donna Nook airfield, mid-1942, are a few examples of the exhibits in just one display hall.

In the same hall, recovered pieces of AE436, a Hampden twin-engine bomber that crashed on Tsatsa Mountain, Norway, in September 1942. These are set out for visitors to view, with the story of how it lay undisturbed until discovered in 1976, along with the remains of its crew. Photographs illustrate its recovery. Additionally, a Merlin engine, and the original wind tunnel model of the Vulcan 'V' bomber that was used for wind tunnel trials, gives one the opportunity to see these magnificent machines close-up.

******

On 4 June, that year, another big day for the Centre dawned. Members of the RAF Escaping Society were visiting and officially opening the ever-growing Escape Museum building.

By the time the Second World War had ended, records showed that a total of 2,803 aircrew had escaped or evaded capture after being shot down over Europe, and made their way safely back to home. Approximately two hundred of these had actually escaped from prisoner-of-war camps – a very difficult and dangerous thing to do. These remarkable feats were almost entirely due to help received from people living in enemy-occupied countries, at great risk to themselves and their families. They supplied food, shelter and, very often, the means to get out of Europe.

"The Escaping Society has devoted its time, money and energy trying to maintain contact with these admirable people on the continent," said Captain Frank Dell, the Society's chairman who was there to perform the opening ceremony by unveiling a commemorative plaque. "We want them to know we have not forgotten what they did for us in those perilous days."

Now a charity, the Society helps those who suffered, or are still suffering, from having been incarcerated in prisoner of war or concentration camps, by giving financial or other forms of assistance. For example, a young girl who was in Auschwitz, an unwilling 'patient' of the infamous Dr Joseph Mengele, was, during the 1980s, given an operation to replace both hips so that she might walk again. The cost of this operation was met by the RAF Escaping Society.

A special guest that day was Madame Hélène Delsaer-Geurts from Belgium, who, as a young woman, had been one of those involved in aiding escapees. She was invited along as a representative of her gallant European countrymen and women.

"It was a hazardous time," Frank Dell said. "One has an undying gratitude to those people."

The duty of an airman is to return to his unit was the instruction given to those young men who served in the RAF. In order to prepare them for the eventuality of being shot down over enemy territory, aircrew were trained, briefed and equipped to avoid capture. For example, they were taught that the first action upon landing was to remove all evidence of their presence by burying or, at the very least, hiding their parachute and Mae West. It was then essential that they develop a plan of movement.

Having survived thus far, it was an undeniable fact that many might be captured by the enemy. If this was the case, they knew it was imperative they should do their utmost to escape in order to continue their part in the war effort. This not only meant they risked their own lives but also those of anyone thought to be aiding them, but they still obeyed this directive and, as we know, many of them did manage to return to their bases.

Here, at the Lincolnshire Aviation Heritage Centre, the Escape Hut is a special tribute housing memorabilia in recognition of the courage and dedication of such escapees and their courageous helpers. With photographs, diagrams, diorama and various mementoes on display, visitors learn how some of these brave people did just as their instructions said, they returned to their units to continue the fight.

The RAF Escaping Society has set up its own showcases amongst the exhibits. Some of the real-life stories include attempts to escape from prisoner-of-war camps. For example, there is detailed information about 'Harry', a three hundred and fifty feet long escape tunnel dug, by hand, thirty feet underground. That amazing feat at Stalag Luft 3 took fifteen months to complete. The story about the famous Wooden Horse, along with a half-scale replica of the original hollow vaulting horse used to mask the activities of the escapees, is graphically explained. Also, 'Albert RN' is present – the dummy made in easily concealed sections by officers in Oflag 4B and used as a replacement for escapees from the prison camp's outside bathing facilities.

Those who were able to evade capture after their damaged aircraft had come down – uninjured aircrew, or those at least still able to walk, would head in a specific direction, hopefully towards help. They would not necessarily remain together, as parachute landings rarely occurred close together, so, once on the ground, it could be each man for himself.

As they would still be wearing their conspicuously alien RAF uniform, the airmen travelled by night – taking care to avoid roads, towns and any other built-up areas. If it was possible to 'obtain' civilian clothing, they could then attempt travelling in daylight. However, they had to be prepared to hide immediately there might be a possibility of detection, whether it was day or night. They each carried an 'escape' kit: maps and compasses for navigation; food tablets, water purifying tablets, chewing gum and chocolate for sustenance; money in francs and guilders.

It was always hoped that aircrew who had been shot down might eventually make contact with friendly civilians – or, even better, be located by one of the Escape Route organisations that operated sensitive intelligence gathering systems. News of a crash, and hence the presence of airmen evading capture, was usually quickly passed to the escape route organisations who could then anticipate the fugitives' movements and mount patrols in the areas where evaders and casualties could be expected.

On entry into an Escape Route, an evader was usually hidden in a 'safe house' whilst The Route team:

a) checked his identity.

b) rendered medical assistance, if necessary.

c) gave the evader a new identity plus the necessary documents: work permits; ration cards, travel permits and identity cards.

d) trained him in his new disguise.

When The Route was ready to move the evader, it would expertly guide him from the 'safe house' along the escape route until he reached, and crossed, a frontier to freedom – so allowing him to return to his unit.

Many stories of those brave allies who helped the evaders are depicted in the Escape Hut, illustrated with photographs of some of the people involved - including two French ladies – Madame M Ugeux (aka Michou) and Madame N Dumont (aka Dedee), later honoured by the French, Belgian, British and American governments. These ladies headed the 'Comet line', a secret organisation that helped two hundred and eighty-eight Allied airmen return home to re-enter the fight.

A fascinating, emotive and thought provoking example of heroism that can be read is one behind the tale of 'the coat'. The actual jacket – donated by Elsie Marachaf, a Comet helper – can be seen in the Escape Hut, too, but that is another story.

Amongst numerous other related instances of escape is a documented and illustrated display concerning The Goldfish Club, an organisation of aircrew who survived ditching in the sea.

The Escape Museum is dedicated to the memory of all these brave people, both living in, and escaping from, occupied Europe during World War II. Interestingly, one of the Centre's guides is Ron Emeny, who, as a Flight Sergeant, was one of the last two people to escape from Europe.

The official opening of the Escape Hut over, the question on everyone's lips was, "What's next?"

The answer was just what they wanted to hear. *Just Jane* could fire on two engines, and a third was already being worked on, so Fred and Harold decided it was time for another exciting step to be taken – a short taxi run.

CHAPTER XIV

Celebrating half a century

Meanwhile, work had also been carried out on the third – number one – engine. Stripped down, she, too, was soon ready for ground running after a series of initial short test runs.

Saturday, 22 April 1995 was the day chosen to celebrate *Just Jane*'s fiftieth birthday – and the first public taxi run. Prior to this, she had undergone a few trial runs to ensure everything worked as it should, that the brakes would not fail, and that she would turn and go wherever she was supposed to go. There had been one or two hiccups, but generally speaking, everything went well.

"I can still clearly remember the look on Fred and Harold's faces when, on 24 March 1995, I released the brakes and, for the first time in more than twenty years, NX611 rolled forward, just about thirty feet, under her own power, on the concrete in front of the hangar," said Mike Chatterton later.

Ian also remembers how both he and Mike must have looked when, during one of the trial runs, the cable from the brake lever to the control valve became disconnected at one end, and suddenly they were out of control. For a few desperate moments, Ian, on his hands and knees on the cockpit floor, fought to manually operate the lever on the brake control valve. He succeeded. The aircraft responded immediately and safely, much to their relief.

"I feel very humbled, and honoured, to be asked to operate a second Lancaster. To be able to both fly P474, the *City of Lincoln* and taxi *Just Jane* is incredible, "said Mike. "The big difference is that this aircraft has been restored entirely by private individuals with great enthusiasm and dedication – the Coningsby Lancaster is a military aircraft, it works under military regulations with military assistance. The atmosphere is different here, too – we're always surrounded by friends and family."

Mike's father, present for the occasion, had flown from this very airfield exactly fifty years before.

"I have a lump in my throat every time I see Mike. I have a *bon mot* for how I feel when I see my son in a Lancaster – when you get to be seventy-five, the flame of life is flickering a little bit, but by no means dead, and nothing can be better calculated to make the embers glow than to see your son doing something you did yourself."

Despite cold, pouring rain and a low ceiling of heavy grey cloud, a huge crowd appeared to witness the event. But, as Mike commented, even though it was daytime and not night, the weather was still reminiscent of the dreadful conditions when wartime operations had to be carried out, regardless.

"Safety aspects were different, then," he remarked. "The idea was to get the job done. They expected to lose aircraft then."`

But safety was a major consideration on this day. Before the taxi run, Mike gathered together those who were going to be forming the team acting as ground crew and those responsible for crowd control. His experience working with the BBMF and being involved with air shows had taught him the absolute necessity for ensuring everyone knew the importance of their roles and how to carry them out most efficiently.

Once satisfied they were all ready, Mike dismissed the teams to their posts and made his way over to the waiting Lancaster. Ian, who would be in the cockpit with him, felt a mixture of fear and exhilaration coursing through him as he accompanied Mike through the chattering expectant throng massed around the perimeter rope.

'If anything should happen…' he thought. But by the time he was in place, his optimism had resurfaced and he felt confident *Just Jane*'s performance would be exemplary.

The rain continued to pour down, but umbrellas up, head coverings and waterproofs in place, the Lancaster's huge throng of admirers emerged from the shelter of various buildings around the airfield to crowd the perimeter rope. Cameras and camcorders were poised to record the forthcoming unique event. The weather was ignored.

Once at the aircraft's side, Ian declared he had "no worries as such, but not having done it with this aircraft before, it's obviously unnerving. You don't know how it's going to react when it's moving – vibration, and such."

But he need not have worried.

When her three engines were all fired up, albeit one still having all her workings on view, they settled into a steady thrum and then, gently she glided forward – moving under her own power with ease. As she passed along the short stretch of runway towards the edge of the Centre's boundary, many of her younger watchers recovered from their initial amazement at what they were witnessing and ran alongside her, behind the rope barrier.

When she reached the end of the run, Mike turned her and, with her tail facing the open countryside, nose towards the way she had just travelled, he held her there for a few minutes before moving off on the return journey.

Safely back in front of the hangar, her engines idled, and then were switched off.

Just Jane was now only the third Lancaster aircraft in the world capable of moving under her own power.

It was still raining heavily, but the smiles of delight from the crowd, their cheers and whistles, only too obviously showed that no one cared in the slightest about the bad weather.

Another memorable taxi run took place after a special VE Day service in the hangar on Sunday 7 May, a day before the actual VE anniversary date – 8 May. Fifty years before, on that date, Victory in Europe day was celebrated by the Allies. Mike was in the pilot's seat, accompanied by Ian.

"Today was another big notch for us, another first," Mike said when he climbed down from the Lancaster. "The engines have been refined. They're right on cue, just right. I was expecting it to require a lot more power but moving off didn't need much power, nor did the turn – she came around beautifully. It felt good, and very similar to the Coningsby Lancaster. When we actually taxi our Lanc over at Coningsby, the outboard engines are idle, so there's very little power. The forward thrust we've got with *Just Jane* and her working engines is similar.

"When I taxi, the outboard engines are idle, so that's about 600 rpm or so; but they still provide a little bit of power there. I found, today, with the normal settings on the inboards at about 1200, I actually used my brakes a bit more than usual. So I'm going to have to alter my technique and have less power on the inboards."

Mike admitted that, initially, when *Just Jane* first did the taxi runs, he was a little wary of the braking system, because it tended to lose pressure and, hence, braking power.

"But now they've been worked on," he said. "When we first started doing this, we'd have gone from about 400 psi back down to about 200, which is very close to the limits. Today, we only lost about 50psi, partly because I'm getting used to handling the aircraft and I can just put in a bit of brake input when I need to; but it's because the brake system is top notch as well."

"I've had a few taxi runs, now," he continued, "but we're always very cautious – especially with lots of people watching. It makes it even more nerve-wracking. The more there are, the less predictable they are. I've learned that from my air show days with the BBMF, so I'm always very wary of the public and keep my eye on them."

Ian agreed that, basically, there had been no significant problems. His main concern, beforehand, was the braking system, because, as he said, "…if the brakes go, you've got no control over the aircraft. But they were fine."

The third engine did overheat and not behave quite as it should have, but he was happy they had managed to get this one run out of it. For the second taxi of the day, a couple of hours later, that engine would not be powered up.

"We're going to have to take the radiator off and have a look at the cooling system," he told Fred and Harold. "Apart from that, everything else works great."

He declared that, for him, it was the "best feeling in the world in a moving Lanc. I can't believe – last year it was just an aeroplane, it stood there doing nothing, and now, thirteen months later, we're taxiing it. The engines are behaving better and better; there's no smoke, nothing. It's doing what it was designed to do."

Roy, too, has a vital responsibility as a member of the Lancaster's team. His role is to 'marshall' the aircraft all the way round her taxi run, ensuring she avoids hitting anything or allows a wheel to come off the concrete. He admitted the only worry he had this particular time was when she was going through the gap at the end of her run. "There's a tower there on the other side of the hen-house, there, you see – and that was a little bit iffy. But once you did that, coming back was a doddle really."

Comments from the visitors included, "Fantastic!" Marvellous!" and "Better every time we come."

No one thought to ask the chickens what they thought about it all.

CHAPTER XV

Moving on…

Work started immediately on Number 4 engine. Reconditioning this one took nearer eight weeks instead of the seven it had taken for the other three.

"There was a problem with one of the radiators," explained Ian. "It leaked quite badly. We sent it to Cambridge, to Jerry Marshall who looks after the BBMF and Duxford radiators."

The repair took about five weeks, but the engine, itself, only took six.

"We'd got used to doing them."

The whole job was completed on 11 July and so, on 13 July 1995, the start up of the fourth and final engine was able to take place, with Ian at the controls.

******

There were the usual puffs of white smoke as a result of the engine and its exhaust system having been coated with inhibiting oil to prevent corrosion during her long years of immobility, then away she went. But it was obvious to the watchers that Ian, who was in the pilot's seat, was not too pleased about something.

Afterwards, as he came out of the aircraft and sat on the steps at her doorway, he nevertheless assured Fred and Harold,

"There's nothing wrong with the engine. I only gave it low rpm – about 600 - else it would have run away. I know I can stop it – it stopped fairly quick."

He then decided to run all four engines together; continually reassuring Fred there was nothing seriously wrong with the newly restored number 4 engine. Climbing back inside and taking the controls, he said, via the intercom between him and Roy, "Let's try again,"

"What order? One, two, three, four?"

"No. Three, two, one, four."

"Right. Tell me when you're ready."

This time, one by one, all four engines were fired up and seemed to be running smoothly. When Ian eventually came back to the doorway, he sat on the steps with a look of glee on his face and told Fred, Harold and Roy,

"Went well. A few electrical problems, but it went all right".

He stepped to the ground, and walked away from the aircraft to cheers and applause of the crowd.

"What about Roy?" someone shouted, pointing out the fact there had been two members of *Just Jane*'s engineering team responsible for what they had all just witnessed.

The applause started up again, and Roy took his credit with a happy, if somewhat embarrassed smile.

They had done it – now all four of *Just Jane*'s engines were in working order.

******

Later, Ian and Roy had a quick discussion with Fred and Harold.

"It could be a loose wire," said Ian, explaining the reason he had looked a little worried earlier. "The other thing that did worry me slightly were the mags[1]. It didn't switch off on the mags. Fortunately, the fuel shut-off works! If it's got no fuel, it'll stop. Everything's OK. We'll sort the electrics out tomorrow."

Mike's response to the event was a happy one.

"It was quite remarkable, today. "We've gone through all these different stages now: one engine running, then two engines running, and then three; then the taxiing and the official VE Day taxi. As I stood out here, watching the fourth engine tick over [as it was a static display, Ian was at the controls] with one, two and three already going, I could stand back and watch it. It meant more to me than anything else up to now because they've already reached the stage where it looks like they've got a wartime Lanc from the East Kirkby era."

CHAPTER XVI

What's in a name?

VJ Day (15 August 1945) was when victory over Japan was celebrated by the Allies – although the Japanese did not actually sign the surrender document until 2 September 1945, aboard the USS *Missouri* riding at anchor in Tokyo Bay. The fiftieth anniversary of this event was actually celebrated at East Kirkby two days early, on Sunday, 13 August, when a memorial service was held in the hangar, with *Just Jane* as backdrop.

Afterwards, her four Merlin engines – all now fully 'cowled up' and ship-shape - confidently roared out in victory as the Lancaster rolled down the short runway from her hangar, her nose gazing ever skywards as though yearning to soar aloft into the heavens once more. Every one of her devoted fan club that attended that day could see she was glad to be moving.

While she taxied along, the sound of an aircraft overhead drew the attention of the spectators. From nearby RAF Coningsby, the BBMF Lancaster, Spitfire and Hurricane flew overhead, in formation, acknowledging the triumph of the brave but lonely Lancaster on the ground below.

It was an emotional few minutes as eyes gazed skywards in admiration, before returning once more to their beloved *Just Jane*. She seemed to state, 'I am here, I am alive – one day I, too, will be up there.'

Eventually, peace settled over the gathering, and the East Kirkby Lancaster was, once again, standing in proud majesty amongst her adoring fans who wandered around her, touching those parts of her they could reach: fuselage, tail planes, rear gun turret and the tips of her mighty propellers, or looking through the doorway to her interior. They admired and commented, the older visitors speaking wisely, backed by knowledgeable experience, while the younger folk gazed in wonder as they tried to imagine how it must have been, taking to the air in such a machine. Stories were busily swapped – some personal, others that had been passed down from family and friends.

******

Mike Chatterton had had a unique choice offered him for that day.

"It was an awkward decision," he explained, watching the crowds gathering around the Lancaster. "I could have flown the Coningsby Lanc or come here to taxi this one. I'm pleased with the decision I made. Instead, Rick Groombridge[1] flew *The City of Lincoln*.

"There's no-one else to taxi *Just Jane* yet, but we've got a few possibles in mind. They'll have to be trained up, then Fred will have more flexibility."

Fred remarked how nice a feeling it was to see all four of her engines running.

"There was a bit of a hiccup at the beginning," he commented. "When you start an engine up after twenty-three years, you've got to be careful how much petrol you pump into the carburettor and the system. It's got to be done gradually or it'll cause a fire. But it did start up eventually – took about three minutes."

It had taken just eighteen months for Ian and Roy to get all four engines running properly. As Fred remarked, "It's uncanny the speed it's all been done."

Harold was happy. "It's looking good," he said. "You can feel the power building up when he revs the engines up. It's a great feeling. We've nearly gone as far as we can with it on the ground. It's really come alive. You can see it wants to fly."

That last statement is one that had been on everyone's lips. People keep asking, "Will she fly again?" But the brothers are being coy about this.

"I'm sure she'll fly one day," says Fred, as Harold nods in agreement. "Once we've set plans in motion, that'll be it. We'll just keep going until we've completed the project."

No promises are made, not at any time, as they both agree that although they would like to see their Lancaster in the air again, flying as she was meant to do, it is, to use their words – "a big decision". She would have to pass a rigorous testing throughout, including her airframe, before an airworthiness certificate could be issued.

Also, as Fred once said, if they did decide she should fly again, there would be no point in her making just the one flight – she would have to remain airworthy. To do this would be a great expense – but not beyond the means of the Aviation Heritage Centre and its ardent supporters. The one big drawback to actually going ahead is that once she is an airworthy machine again, there is always the possibility she could crash. It may be a remote possibility, but it could happen.

That would be the end of *Just Jane*, which, in turn, would be the end of the museum. The whole package is centred round this wonderful Lancaster. Frustrating it may be, but it is right that Fred and Harold should be wary of taking that momentous step.

******

Six days later, on 19 August 1995, NX611 – *Just Jane* - was given an additional name. At a special ceremony, she was officially christened the *City of Sheffield* by the Lord Mayor of that city.

Why was NX611, *Just Jane*, named the *City of Sheffield?* Well, of course, there is already a *City of Lincoln* – the BBMF Lancaster at RAF Coningsby. Also, as the Lord Mayor, Councillor David Heslop, in his address to the hundreds of people who attended the ceremony, said, "This Lancaster was named in memory of more than two thousand people who worked in the Sheffield steelworks – English Steel, Firth Brown, Samuel Fox and other great names of steel in Sheffield - during the war. They made the castings, casings, and so on, for the Bouncing Bombs and others, and aircraft parts, including parts for Lancasters. For example, the Merlin crankshafts which power this 'plane were made at the River Don Works which is now a part of Forgemasters; and that's a tribute for those who suffered through the bombing raids on that city.

"This 'plane is very much a part of Sheffield. We, in Sheffield, very much look forward to the day this 'plane will fly over Sheffield."

As far as Fred and Harold's sentiments are concerned, they say, "We lived not far from Sheffield when war broke out, only about sixteen miles away, and remember the blitz there, caused by the German raids. Then there were all the coalmines –not only in Sheffield, but also in north Nottinghamshire. They did a lot for the war effort, too, producing the fuel for the steelworks. We've got a lot of respect for what those miners did. Today, there's a million people live in Sheffield - calling our Lancaster after the city, we hope it will make them proud."

"It's personal thing," agreed Harold. "She will still be called *Just Jane* – that's what everyone knows her as. The city of Sheffield is only sixty-five miles up the road from here. We've not agreed anything with Sheffield city, but we hope it'll be of mutual benefit."

******

Dutifully, *Just Jane* carried out her, by now routine, couple of taxiing trips that afternoon, complete with passengers who delighted in the novel experience of riding inside a moving Lancaster. At the far end of the run, after she had turned to face the way from which she come, Mike held her steady for a few minutes and increased power to her inboard engines.

The Merlins roared out. Excited spectators saw the grass behind her lying completely flattened and a huge cloud of dust flying up into the air. Anything not fastened down tightly was also dislodged, including a two of the high chain-link fence panels that normally acted as a division between the Centre and the area where Panton brothers' chicken sheds are situated. Forced backwards by the blast, they surrendered to the mighty force and dropped, flattened on the ground.

Suddenly, the noise and dust settled, the engines regained their controlled, steady thrumming, and the magnificent Avro Lancaster began her return journey.

"The engines are done, brakes are done, and all the electrics done, everything in the cockpit is right. We're finished now – unless we try to get it into the air," said Fred afterwards. "I'm sure it will fly one day, but I wouldn't like to put a time or a date on that. Before it can do that, it's got to be assessed with the Aerospace people, and that could take three months for them to go over it and give a true costing to do it. It would be a three-man team – for which they would charge. It's a costly item just to reassess, but necessary to know how much it'll cost to go down that road."

Changing the subject, unwilling to commit himself to the question of will she/won't she fly again, he went on, "It's fifty years since four Merlin engines ran on this airfield. It's a nostalgic feeling. It's put a soul back into the 'plane – if that's the right word."

After a moment's thought, he added quietly, "There's no reason why it shouldn't fly."

Should the Panton brothers decide to go ahead, adequate finances will have to be in place. There will be the cost of the inspection of her airframe and main spars – a job that will have to be done by British Aerospace and, although she has been renovated to very high standards and is maintained in excellent working order, her airframe will have to be transported to the old Avro manufacturing base at Chadderton, in Manchester, for a thorough overhaul. Once she has been passed as airworthy again, there will of course be the considerable cost of keeping her in that condition.

As Fred said, "Once you go down that road, you've got to fly it for quite a lot of years."

But ask any of the pilots who taxi her – they will readily agree: *Just Jane* is a Lancaster straining to fly every time her brakes are released and she rolls along the runway.

Once again, the brothers make known their thoughts.

Fred: "There's still four hundred flying hours left in those engines; they're in mint condition. We'll make our minds up between now and January if we'll fly it. First week in January, you'll have an answer. If we do, it'll take eighteen months at most to get her ready."

Harold: "We'll have to have a long, hard think. It'll be nice to see it fly. She's made to fly – you can see when she's taxiing, her tail end bouncing. She's saying, 'Let me go, why can't I go? I'm airborne, more-or-less. Take those brakes off. I'll show you whether I can fly or not."

Fred: "Anyway, the engines are not started over the winter. She's going to bed now,"

CHAPTER XVII

Winter maintenance and another new year

Just Jane is always returned to her hangar for the winter months, although the museum remains open and visitors may go into the hangar to see her. During the winter of 1995 to 1996, her engines were inhibited and her outer skin thoroughly cleaned and given a coating of special protective lubricant to guard against corrosion resulting from exposure to the elements.

"I bought a book on the Lanc in a car boot sale and when I read about it, I decided I wanted to clean this aircraft," explained Michael Francis from the company who volunteered to undertake the job that season. He and his colleague, Tony, used their specialist skills and materials to ensure the work was properly carried out.

"The job is dirty, smelly, but enjoyable when it's an historic aircraft."

Fred did the cleaning himself, once upon a time; knowing the importance of keeping the aircraft's rivets moist and preventing corrosion.

"It used to take me a week," he said, "but it only took them about two days!"

The engineers made use of the time the aircraft was idle to work on the hydraulic system, connecting up the lines for the bomb doors and flaps so that they could work as they were meant to. Before this, they had been fixed down. This entailed replacing about one hundred and forty feet of pipework, in all.

"The Perspex had all gone milky so we had to replace that, too," explained Ian. "We got some Lexan from a Grimsby company – it's used on helicopters. All the main Perspex was done."

******

When the BBMF team from RAF Coningsby approached the East Kirkby team for help in obtaining a new nosepiece for PA474 that winter, it was agreed that *Just Jane*'s should be used as a template.

It is the only original left in the world.

"We removed the nosepiece and BBMF transported it to London to a company there (it's gone now) to have a new one made," said Ian. "They left us with a small plastic bubble as a temporary replacement. It was about six or seven weeks before we had ours back. But as it was cheaper to buy two new nosepieces at the same time, we were given one – so we had a new one for *Just Jane*.

"We fitted ours before BBMF. They wanted to watch how we did it, and for us to make the mistakes, but we didn't make any!"

It took the East Kirkby engineers only half a day to fit the new nose, after drilling holes for its fitments.

******

Also, ironically, the task of reupholstering inside the aircraft was undertaken during that period by German-born William (Bill) Seidel, who arrived in Britain as a prisoner of war, staying on and marrying a Lincolnshire lady. Now a Lincolnshire resident, the former German infantryman put his talents to use when he successfully restored all the aircraft's leather upholstery.

******

The aircraft's wheels were also taken off, so that the braking system could be thoroughly overhauled. RAF Coningsby helped out by examining and testing out the brake drums.

"We have a very good relationship with Coningsby," says Ian. "They have a lot of stuff they won't use on their aircraft, and we sometimes have some good stuff going spare, so we can swap things about."

Once the hubs were tested, they were refitted. Then Ian and Roy made sure the aircraft pneumatic system was operational, all the air lines were sealed, the valves correctly fitted and the system was successfully pressure tested.

******

Just before Christmas, a full band accompanied a huge congregation, which filled the hangar for a traditional Christmas Carol Service. It was a special evening, with smiles all round. At the end of the service, Father Christmas appeared with his sack of 'goodies', while a 'snowstorm' blew in through the open hangar doors. It was artificial snow, so no one had any trouble getting home afterwards.

******

The hangar at East Kirkby is not just home to NX611. Static displays of WWII artefacts surround this famous old lady of the skies. It is the setting for a wide and infinitely varied collection of aviation memorabilia, including British, American and German aircraft components, flight clothing and model aircraft and vehicles. They come from numerous different types of aircraft, many recovered by the Lincolnshire Aircraft Recovery Group, through to a display by the Shackleton Association. Although the First World War is also represented, embodied by both American Naval and British RAF memorabilia, the majority of artefacts and memorabilia exhibited are from WWII.

Spacious, clean and with carefully arrayed displays containing photographs and explanatory narrative, the hangar's plethora of immensely interesting artefacts can create an initial feeling of: "Where on earth shall I start looking?" One of the first items to be seen is the Visitors' Book, placed near the entrance and in which men, women and children from all over the world have written such comments as:

"I'm a German and was in the German flack [sic]. It was always my ambition, without any animosity, to come face-to-face with a Lanc..." (Dated August 1999).

"I was five years old when the war started. We lived in London's East End...we shared a steel indoor shelter with a Catholic Irish lady who prayed whilst an air raid was on, but she would sprinkle her prayer with the most obscene swear words to describe the raiders..." (Also dated August 1999).

Each display case has a different story to tell, ranging from examples of the funnier side of life in Bomber Command to the tragic events that changed ordinary people's lives forever. Unreservedly, though, all depict unquestionably true heroism shown by the people of that war-torn era. Faces of young men, many of whom were barely out of their boyhood but now long gone, look out from these displays in photographs, each having played his own small, but important, part for the cause of freedom.

The many thousands of poignant missives sent by the Air Ministry to families when young airmen went missing, only too often to be followed by later confirmation of the death of that loved one, are represented by a few surviving examples here, in the hangar. This, for instance:

"Madam,

I am commanded by the Air Council to express to you their regret on hearing your husband, Sergeant Stanley Charles Walton, Royal Air Force, is missing as the result of air operations on the night of 10/11 April, 1945, where a Lancaster aircraft in which he was flying as flight engineer set out to bomb Leipzig and failed to return. This does not necessarily mean that he is killed or wounded, and if he is a prisoner of war he should be able to communicate with you in due course..."

(Dated 11 April 1945)

Another letter, sent at the same time, assured her:

"...the family allowance and allotment of 60s. 0d a week at present is payment to you..."

Young Mrs Walton was eventually to learn that her husband had been killed.

******

Visitors can see original notes for both instructors and students of Air Navigation. They make fascinating reading. Young men, who would soon be plotting aircraft routes through the night skies over enemy territory and seemingly featureless waters, were only too aware of how vital their knowledge and skills were to the safety of the whole crew. Thus, their studies would consist of such topics as the importance of knowing the stars, knowing why the Plough never sets for an observer in Northern Europe, and how to read a Cloud Atlas.

Newspaper articles of the period abound, giving us an insight into the day-to-day reporting of the conflict – not just in this country, but throughout Europe; whilst items donated by ex-RAF personnel and their families – from diaries to log books – reveal the more personal side of these fighting men and women.

Bomb trolleys and the dambuster bomb, salvaged parts of those long-ago doomed aircraft – including a Shackleton (roomier than the Lancaster and having its main spar under the floor), a Spitfire and Blenheim IV, as well as accounts of how these aircraft came to crash', are on display. Opportunities to sit in some of the rescued aircraft sections, such as the crew compartment housed in the nose section of a Canberra jet bomber, show only too well the cramped and spartan conditions those young men endured whilst airborne. Trying the navigator's ejection seat for size is an eye-opener.

Photographs, along with the history and exploits of East Kirkby's own Squadrons – No 57 and No 630 – illustrate what it was like to live and work on this airfield during those war years. So, too, is there information and photographs of sister squadrons displayed here.

A central map of Lancaster targets for the period 1942 to 1945 shows the extent of operations carried out by the whole of Bomber Command during that period. A Battle Order and aerial views of various Lincolnshire airfields is on view. The Polish Air Force is remembered here, as are details of 'Operation Manna', the lifesaving mission of airlifting food to the Dutch people, who were starving towards the end of the Second World War. So, too can be seen details of the sinking of the *'Tirpitz'* during a daring daylight bombing raid, illustrated via pictures and explanatory notes – including reproductions of the original combat photographs.

Wonderful collections of miniature model vehicles, on loan from Bengurian Models of East Keal, Spilsby, include examples of a large number of the different types of transport familiar to those who lived and worked during the 1940s. They include British transport vehicles, heavy prime movers and landing craft; modern British soft skin vehicles; tanks and armoured vehicles dating from between 1948 to 1995; and a number of German, American, Israeli and Russian military vehicles.

Two 'commemorative windows' made in honour of 617 (Dambusters) Squadron by Grimsby man, John Freear, are on show, one of which celebrated the fiftieth anniversary of the Squadron's formation. The other honours the fiftieth anniversary of the famous Dams raid.

******

Leaving the hangar and going to any part of the Centre's ground area, sentinels in the form of trees are to be found, each with a plaque announcing it had been planted by the family and/or friends of either individual aircrew or the complete crew of an aircraft lost on operations. There is, of course, one for Chris Panton.

******

As a celebration of the new millennium, the University of Greenwich inaugurated the planting of a line of trees right across the United Kingdom on the Greenwich Meridian Line – at 0° Longitude.

This Millennium Tree Line actually passes across the airfield at East Kirkby and, consequently, is now represented by saplings that were planted on 24 February 1998. A plaque commemorating this event bears the words:

"To all those who crossed the Meridian for our freedom of body and spirit.

May their effort never be wasted."

CHAPTER XVIII

Memorable visitors

The following January came and went, but still the brothers had not made up their mind as to whether or not *Just Jane* would be made ready to fly.

Between 1996 and 2001, her engines were run periodically and kept in tip-top condition. As usual, she had many visitors of note, some of who remain particularly clear in the memory.

'Jacko' Jackson, on one of his visits to the Centre, recollected the first time he came across NX611.

"I was stationed in Singapore in 1965," he said. "It [*Just Jane*] was being ferried to England. One of my secondary jobs out there was to look after visiting people, so I looked after the crew of this aeroplane. Then I also came across it at Blackpool, and I saw it many times at Scampton. The last chap who ever flew it was the great aerobatic pilot Neil Williams – to Blackpool.

"It was quite emotional when I saw all four engines running. I've many happy memories of it."

******

In August 1996, there was a 1940s style dance in the hangar, and the Centre's first air show was held. In early September, Bill Reid VC came along to taxi *Just Jane* with 'Jacko' Jackson, and representatives from the American Smithsonian Association were made welcome.

******

Then came the Germans, on 12 July 1997. They were welcome visitors, these aircrew veterans who were taking part in the scheme entitled 'Flightpath to Friendship and Reconciliation'. It was the first time they had seen a Lancaster aircraft since meeting them in combat over Germany during World War Two.

Some of them spoke English, but those who did not were able to recount their experiences through the German-speaking ex-RAF author, Peter Hinchcliffe. Standing around *Just Jane* on the apron outside her hangar, they all had much to say about their experiences when attacking Lancasters. One admitted that they – the German aircrews - would not have been in as much awe of this type of aircraft had they had the opportunity to see one as they were now seeing *Just Jane*.

During those dark days and, particularly, nights, these men had taken part in deadly aerial combats with Lancasters in the skies over Europe, when the British heavy night-bombing raids on German cities posed a fearsome threat to them. They explained how they would shoot down a bomber, such as the Lancaster.

"We carried, up in top of the Messerschmitt 110 fuselage, cannon that fired upwards," said one. "We could come up astern of the bomber where we wouldn't be seen because we'd be against the background below. These machines were painted grey, difficult to see. We would gradually move up into position beneath the Lancaster – maybe thirty to fifty metres – and through a sight on top of the cannon, we could position the x between the fuselage and the inboard engine, sometimes between two engines.

"It was a lethal method," he continued gravely. "Not suspected by the RAF for a long time. But a touch of the button was enough to destroy a Lancaster because it hit the fuel tank."

One German was obviously distressed as he relived those nights of more than half a century before. His name was Hans Gajewski.

"These poor boys in here," he said, reaching up and tapping the side of *Just Jane*, "they didn't know. It was like execution. They never saw me. You were the winner if you were below them. The poor buggers, they never saw me. They didn't know."

His face twisted in grief as he saw in his mind's eye the picture he was trying to describe.

"I'm sorry to say, they were like executed. I put the lever over and six guns go through…"

He stopped, choked up.

"One fell on top of me afterwards. I didn't eat…"

That was it. He dissolved into silent tears and turned away to hide his face against the giant aircraft, sister to those he once helped destroy.

******

Later, when *Just Jane*'s four Merlins sent out their own reminder of those horrific nights, the sound of PA474's engines drew closer and all eyes looked upwards. The *City of Lincoln* flew over in salute, circled a few times, and then left again.

The Germans all smiled, perhaps feeling a little more at peace.

******

There was another special visitor that same day. It had taken Fred a long time to locate her, but he finally did and, very proudly invited her to come along to visit her namesake. It was Christabel Leighton-Porter, the original 'Just Jane'. As a young woman during the 1940s, she was invited to model for Norman Pett, the comic-strip artist, as the beautiful blonde who was always accompanied by her dachshund, Fritz. The character, Jane, had wonderful adventures which somehow always seemed to involve her losing much of her clothing, and took her romping through the war years and well into the 1950s. The comic strip was published in *The Daily Mirror* newspaper.

Wearing a suit of delicate pink and a pearl necklace, her hair the traditional 'Just Jane' blonde, the now elderly Miss Leighton-Porter was happy to address the crowd, telling them how pleasantly surprised she had been upon arriving, to find there was so much more to the Lincolnshire Aviation Heritage Centre than one aircraft and a few onlookers, as she had expected.

******

Another very welcome visitor was Harry Cooper, one of Chris Panton's surviving crewmates. He came across to this country from Vancouver, Canada, with some of his family to meet Chris's younger brothers again, fifty years after his post-war visit to their parents. He rode in the cockpit as *Just Jane* taxied, looking down at the taxiway and around the airfield, and – although in a different aircraft from that in which he had flown more than fifty years before – obviously reliving his youth.

Later, as he carefully descended the steps to the ground, he commented, "We could jump down from the Halifax."

His sons, Dave and Bob, were moved by the experience. They admitted that their father had never talked much about his experiences during the war years, but this visit had helped him to 'open up'.

"It's brought us closer together," they said. "Wish our sister was here."

Fred's comment summed up his feelings quite succinctly, "Best week of my life to meet up with him."

******

In September 1997, a 57 Squadron Lancaster engine recovered in Holland was brought to East Kirkby, back to the airfield from where it had made its final journey.

******

The airfield and its hangar had, by now, become a popular venues for music concerts – Irish singer Mary Duff, drew an audience of 1,100, and the Syd Lawrence Band entertained diners with a selection, particularly of Glenn Miller's music from the war years.

Night-time taxiing events - shows that enabled the Lancaster to be seen in its natural and proper environment – were originally an experiment, but so popular did they become that the displays were further developed with the aid of fireworks, smoke-producing equipment, the simulated sound of ack-ack guns and explosions as mock attacks by German fighter-bombers were staged.

So spectacular have these types of display proved that they have been repeated on a number of occasions.

CHAPTER XIX

A place of peace

The East Kirkby airfield's multi-denominational chapel was first opened to the public on 29 January 1999. This was followed by an official unveiling ceremony on Saturday 10 July, that same year. The chapel was dedicated to all aircrew of 57 and 630 Squadrons who had served at East Kirkby during World War II. Following the dedication, a commemorative address was delivered by Marshal of the Royal Air Force, Sir Michael Beetham, GCB, CBE, DFC, AFC, DL.

Planned and constructed using the shell of the airfield's original USAF fire station, the Aviation Heritage Centre's Memorial Chapel contains a Roll of Honour, furnishings, pulpit, pews, organ, communion rail and other items taken from the disused Methodist Chapel (built in 1842) at Lusby, near Spilsby. In September 1999, it saw its first public service when a wedding ceremony was held there, followed by a reception in the main hangar.

A rich, deep blue carpet invites the visitor to walk into the serene building and take time looking around at framed religious prints, poems and badges on the walls. But most eye-catching of all are the rolls of honour on the chapel's inner north and south walls, listing in gold leaf lettering on two massive polished wooden display boards all those who gave their lives whilst operating out of RAF East Kirkby during World War II. These names are also alphabetically listed in the two Books of Remembrance kept in the building – one book each for 57 and 630. To the right of each name is the date of that person's demise, along with the place of internment and grave number, or the location of the commemorative stone, as the case may be.

The numbers of personnel based at East Kirkby airfield who died are:

No 57 Squadron		No 630 Squadron	
RAF	349	RAF	301
RAAF	40	RAAF	29
RCAF	43	RCAF	43
RNZAF	8	RNZAF	11
SAAF	1	SAAF	1
USAAF	3	USAAF	1
RNorAF	3		

It is also noted that a number of non-aircrew station personnel lost their lives during the same period.

CHAPTER XX

The makings of a star

When Fred and Harold gave their permission for the BBC to use their Lancaster in the filming of a forthcoming television production, entitled *Night Flight*, they set themselves and their team quite a task to get things ready. The aircraft would be used to represent a working World War Two Lancaster bomber, necessitating her making taxi runs with her tail end lifting off the ground as though she was about to actually take off. Getting this right meant some serious practising, and the place to do that was not on her usual taxi run but half a mile away on the old runway extension.

Special tracking was laid down between the concrete taxiway and the end of the old runway allowing her to cross from the one to the other and back, for the initial trial, which took place on 14 February. On the morning of that day, *Just Jane*, now painted in camouflage and squadron markings appropriate to those worn by her fellow operational Lancasters of the wartime era, was towed by a tractor to the start point of her journey down the 3,800 foot long runway.

******

With Mike at the controls, and Ian inside the cockpit with him, they carried out a number of test runs.

"For the first one," Ian explained, "the engines were basically ticking over at 1200 rpm to make sure the aircraft stayed under control and didn't veer off to one side. On the second run, the engines were at about 1600 rpm and there was more speed. She behaved herself. For the third run, all four engines were at zero boost, generating 2300 rpm, approximately. The tail was still down. Mike got up more speed to check stability. After this run, the brakes unexpectedly overheated, so she had to be shut down.

"This was because, during the taxi runs, Mike had been testing them – hardish braking at the end of each run to ensure she stopped. Before this, we had not been able to bed them. Initially, low-speed stopping took over a thousand feet – no wonder they overheated. They cooled down over lunch.

"On the fourth run, Mike gave her almost full boost on the inboards and zero boost on the outboards. That was the first time the tail came up, halfway down the runway. We could see the runway ahead of us – the tail was up, so the nose came down. I was controlling the throttles, while Mike was doing all the hard work with the brakes, the steering, etcetera. When the engines were throttled back to idle, the tail came down and she was on three wheels again, then Mike braked and we taxied back."

For the next run, the inboards were set at plus-6, the outboards were at zero. As soon as the tail came up, Ian's job was to find out what throttle setting was required to keep it up without generating too much speed.

"We found plus-6 to start with," he said, "and then zero boost on all four engines during the run, and moving the throttles just to keep it in a flying attitude while still trying to keep the speed down."

By now, the two men were settling into a pattern of control in order to achieve what they wanted. The brakes became properly bedded in and they were stopping safely – in about eight hundred feet - a little closer to the end of the runway.

The sixth and final practise run was carried out with exactly the same throttle settings as the previous one, just to confirm they were correct. The old aircraft reacted in exactly the same way, proving to them they had finally got it right. They were then confident that they would be able to 'perform' on cue for the film crew.

******

A few days later, on the Sunday night, the whole BBC film entourage arrived at East Kirkby. They began preparations for filming the next day and by Wednesday 21 February, were ready to film *Just Jane* demonstrating her latest achievement. That was when the public turned up, all well wrapped up against the cold, bleak, typically February day.

It was not until after lunch that serious filming began. The Lancaster did four runs – two with an actor, dressed in Second World War RAF uniform and strapped in the rear turret, then another two with a cameraman inside the rear turret so that he could film from the rear gunner's perspective.

******

Later, Fred said was pleased with the way things had gone, but he had to admit, "I know Mike Chatterton and the engineers know what they're doing. But I still worry a bit. It's nice to see the back wheel come up – and go down again!"

******

The next day, the Lancaster stood on the runway whilst actors were filmed on the ground around her and inside her. With so many characters in RAF uniform walking around, the scene was quite surreal, inviting the observer to really believe in ghostly happenings on disused airfields. But these characters were real enough. Young men, each playing the part of a Lancaster crewman, clad in full wartime flying gear and feeling in awe of what they represented, commenting on what they felt now they had been inside the aircraft, they said:

"The struggle to even get in the 'plane dressed like this…"

"You have to crouch down, 'cos it's really low, and you have to ease your way backwards."

"The incline goes upwards. It's claustrophobic."

"They must have had nerves of steel to do what they did."

Much of the filming at East Kirkby was shot after dark, using special effects for smoke, wind and fire in order to recreate a Lancaster going off on a bombing raid.

******

When it was all over, filming finished and the airfield given back to the weather, birds and ghosts of airmen, *Just Jane* was towed back to the safety of her hangar. By seven on the Friday night, 23 February 2001, she was inside and settled for the remainder of the winter months. Just as the hangar doors were closing, it started snowing.

CHAPTER XXI

Will she fly again?

That question, "will she fly again?" was first asked by many of her fans, immediately after *Just Jane*'s first engine was started up in April 1994. As each of the other three engines, in turn, have been reconditioned and subsequently proved to run as well as they had when the aircraft was first built in 1945, that same question has become more and more of an issue.

Opinions are divided.

There are those who feel that, in the logical course of events, this Lancaster should be allowed to take to the skies again – back into her natural environment. It is, after all, where she belongs.

Then there are the cautious fans who are satisfied with the progress already made in her restoration. They would prefer to see her remain safely on *terra firma*.

But, of course, the choice is Fred and Harold Panton's. They are the ones who, after almost sixteen years of pursuing their dream – this very Lancaster – brought her to East Kirkby airfield and made her the popular moving star she is today. Although, in his usual unassuming manner, Harold always gives the credit to his brother, "It's all down to Fred, you know. If it wasn't for him, this museum wouldn't be what it is today."

Both of them are adamant, however, that their Lancaster probably will fly again one day. But will it be in their time?

When asked this question in March 2004, Fred answered, "We're still undecided. The last thing we'd want is to see a Lancaster drop out of the sky. We'd never get another. But, after saying that, I'm sure it will fly one day."

So perhaps we should, as they say, watch this space…

NOTES

CHAPTER 1

[1] When the author asked Flight Lieutenant Mike Chatterton what it was like to fly a Lancaster, he replied, "Most modern large aircraft have hydraulic or electronic controls, which means that the pilot just puts an input into a computer or hydraulic system and powerful rams actually move the control surfaces. With the Lancaster, and all aircraft of that vintage, by means of cables, rods, pulleys and chains, the pilot actually moves the control surfaces himself. This means that you can 'feel' the response of the aircraft much better, and 'through the seat of the pants' you can tell what the aircraft is doing long before it shows on the instruments.

"The Lanc [PA474, *City of Lincoln* of the Battle of Britain Memorial Flight] was easy to take off, and a delight to fly. She responded well to the controls in the air and was good fun to display, and had excellent all-round visibility. Because of her size it was quite hard physical work flying a display in the Lanc and, on a warm summer's day, having done two or three display routines inside that 'greenhouse', I would be absolutely saturated in sweat!

"Landing, however, was a different business. Having big, tall fins and fairly large, flat sides, she was affected a lot by cross winds. Wartime airfields usually had two or three runways, so this was not a problem; but these days, most airfields have only one runway and I often found myself, reluctantly, having to cancel flights because the crosswind was out of limits. The tailwheel configuration and big, balloon tyres also meant she was prone to bouncing a lot if you didn't get the roundout just right. I usually found that I managed my biggest bounces in front of the biggest crowds. She would always settle down eventually, so the only damage was to my pride.

"I was very aware that we flew in a totally different environment from that of my father and his colleagues during the [Second World] War. We flew in daytime only; clear of cloud, in good visibility with everyone on our side. The only worries we had were trying to land without too much embarrassment, and where the first beer was coming from. The wartime crews flew in awful weather, with very little experience initially, and with people (including the Royal Navy) trying to shoot them down. They flew over enemy territory for hours on end, and then had to try and find their way back to a blacked out airfield somewhere in Britain. [Preferably the one from which they had started – Author.] My father says he used to fear the weather – the icing, turbulence and freezing conditions, more than he did the enemy. In the very comfortable, secure way of life we have now, it is difficult to imagine how on earth they could control their fear when they went off on such dangerous missions. Then, for the lucky ones who got back, after the huge feeling of relief, they would have to think about going off and doing it all over again.

CHAPTER II

[1] Firsby railway station, near Spilsby, approximately eight miles due east of East Kirkby.

[2] Famed for its underground military town, and its fifteen miles of underground tunnels, Rudloe Manor (no 1 Site) was home to 10 Group. One of several sensitive military installations, it controlled four sector stations, RAF Filton, RAF Middle Wallop, RAF St. Eval and RAF Pembrey. During the Second World War, the Ministry of Aircraft Production built the Beaverbrook underground aircraft factory here for Bristol Aeroplane and other companies. The vast caverns had some 2,250,000 sq ft of space, divided into many smaller chambers. Other local quarries were expanded on and linked together, forming a huge network of tunnels and bunkers, parts of which were used for army storage purposes. An RAF Fighter group HQ (RAF Box), and a communications switching centre were also set up, making the area an important military nerve centre.

Today, still operating in secret, according to the RAF's own web site www.raf.mod.uk, Rudloe Manor is home to No.1 and 6 Signals Units, the MoD Communications Network, Headquarters P&SS [Provost & Security Service] UK RAF P&SS Western Region, and Headquarters Defence Fixed Telecommunications Systems. In a Parliamentary answer on 2nd July 1998, Dr. Reid said RAF Rudloe Manor is an administrative establishment providing accommodation and support for a number of defence organisations, and it includes Hawthorn Central Government war headquarters, to which the cabinet, central government and defence staffs would retreat early in a crisis, leaving London to its fate as the bombs fell.

Rumours abound that Rudloe Manor also has a secret role in monitoring the UFO situation, but there is no really hard evidence for this.

CHAPTER III

[1] *Two Farmers and a Lancaster* (Primetime Video Productions)

[2] *Operation Lancaster* (Primetime Video Productions)

[3] Refers to the second pilot – or, in this case, as Lancasters have only one pilot, the extra crew member, the pilot-in-training, Flight Sergeant W F Rost.

CHAPTER IV

[1] *Two Farmers and a Lancaster* (Primetime Video Productions)

[2] Flight

CHAPTER VI

[1]John Hampshire died April 1990

[2] Sir Patrick Kilvington died in September 1990

[3] *Story of a Lanc'* compiled and written by Brian Goulding, Mike Garbett and John Partridge

[4] Neil Williams died whilst ferrying a Spanish-built Heinkel III from Spain to England in December 1977

CHAPTER VII

[1]NX611's rear turret guns were 0.5-inch calibre; the front turret's were .303.

CHAPTER IX

[1]Now Air Chief Marshall.

CHAPTER XI

[1]*Two Farmers and a Lancaster* (Primetime Video Productions).

[2]A green John Deere tractor is now used.

CHAPTER XIII

[1] The famous 'bouncing bomb', was created by Dr Barnes Wallis, especially for the raid on three of the Ruhr Valley dams on the night of 16/17 May 1943. One of the most talked about feats of courage and ingenuity in the history of the Second World War, it was carried out by a squadron especially formed and trained for the task – No 617, or 'The Dam Busters', and it was the trusty Lancaster aircraft that was chosen to transport the chosen crews with their unique and very special weapons, the 'bouncing bombs'.

Of the twenty-three specially modified BIII Lancasters, nineteen actually survived training to carry out the raid, taking off from RAF Scampton. Three then had to return home because of mechanical problems, leaving sixteen to carry out the raid, each aircraft bearing one 9,250-pound cylindrical 'bouncing bomb'. Approximately five feet long by just over four feet in diameter, the weapon's main explosive charge actually weighed 6,600 lb. Detonated by three hydrostatic pistols at a depth of thirty feet. The bomb was suspended from two V-shaped arms beneath the body of the Lancaster. A hollow, circular track of twenty inches diameter at either end of the bomb's casing mated with disc wheels on the aircraft's arms. A hydraulic motor in the Lancaster's fuselage provided the belt-driven pre-release backspin of 500rpm to the weapon about ten minutes before its release. The bomb would rotate backwards as it was released so that, on impact with the dammed water, it would begin decelerating whilst still bouncing forward through the water. Gradually slowing as it continued its bouncing course (a calculated distance of four hundred to four hundred and fifty yards), it would reach its appointed target and sink down against the dam wall, exploding at a predetermined depth.

In order to ensure accuracy, the aircraft had to fly at exactly sixty feet above the water and at a ground speed of 220mph. The exact height was judged by the coincidence of two spotlights shining on the surface of the water, and the correct range by lining up two uprights on a homemade bombsight with the towers at each side of a dam. It took four bombs to destroy the Mohne Dam, two for the Eder. The final one, the Sorpe – an earth core dam - resisted the one bomb that struck it.

Eight Lancasters and their crews were lost that night: four were shot down by flak, two hit power cables, one ran into a tree, and one was destroyed when its bomb struck the top of the dam wall and exploded beneath the aircraft.

Although the raid was considered a success, having created considerable destruction in the areas downstream of the dams, the survival of the Sorpe meant it failed to achieve its real objective – that of denying water and hydro-electric power to the Ruhr industries.

617 Squadron's Leader, Wing Commander Guy Gibson, was awarded the Victoria Cross.

The practise bombs were painted grey, whilst those actually used were green.

Other famous bombs carried by the Lancaster were the 22,000 lb 'Grand Slam' deep penetration bomb and the 12,000 lb 'Tallboys'. The former was transported by the B1with its strengthened bomb bay for ranges up to 1,550 miles at 200 mph at 15,000 feet. It was the dropping of twenty-eight 'Tallboys' around the *'Tirpitz'* that effectively put that ship out of action.

[2] John Chatterton died 2 March 2004, aged eighty-four.

CHAPTER XIV

[1] Magnetos.

CHAPTER XVI

[1]Squadron Leader Rick Groombridge (Retd), ex-BBMF, 1994 -1996, is one of the three alternative pilots who taxi *Just Jane*. The other two are Squadron Leader Ken 'Jacko' Jackson MBE AFC RAF (Retd) who flew PA474 from 1975 until 1981; and retired Hastings pilot John Sully, who was trained to handle the controls of *Just Jane* by Rick Groombridge.

BIBLIOGRAPHY

- 92 -

RAF *Story of a Lanc (NX611)* compiled and written by Brian Goulding; Mike Garbett; Squadron Leader John Partridge.

www.lancastermuseum.ca/lancs.html

SILKSHEEN – the History of East Kirkby Airfield by Geoff D Copeman.

Lincolnshire Airfields in the Second World War by Patrick Otter.

OTHER EXHIBITS AT LINCOLNSHIRE AVIATION HERITAGE CENTRE

Wander around the outdoor area of the airfield and you will see the actual ground-support vehicles use during the 1940s, including a Fordson WOTI/foamtender (*c* 1941) amongst the collection of tractors from that era, along with bicycles, motorcars and trucks.

Rescued pieces of crashed aircraft include wings, fuel tanks and side panel section of a Vickers Wellington'and an Alvis Leonides 9-cylinder radial engine (520/540hp) as fitted to a Percival P56 Provost training aircraft.

There are parts of propellers from various aircraft, amongst which are photographs including the only known photo of LL667, taken at Witchford in February 1944. Also a Bristol Hercules sleeve valve radial engine, Rolls Royce Derwent jet engines and – to remind us why all this awesome machinery was developed in the first place - bomb racks, bomb shackles, complete with inert bombs and a bomb trolley.

The Brian Nicholls Hampden bomber project

The restoration of Hampden AE 436 is an ongoing venture being undertaken here, at East Kirkby. The story behind its fatal crash, and surviving pieces of its airframe can be seen in Hall No 6. It was on 4 September 1942, that AE 436 – as part of a force of 32 drawn from No 144 and No 455 (RAAF) squadrons – were sent to Russia to help defend the allied convoys operating in the arctic. The flight, almost all in darkness, was to have lasted almost eight hours.

The Percival Proctor IV NP294 is undergoing long-term restoration. In 1939, the Percival Company revised a design of the record breaking Vega Gull aircraft, to meet an Air Ministry specification for a three-seat communications aircraft.

Hall No 7 is the workroom where the public is invited to see the Hampden restoration project in progress, as well as a display of Wellington parts.

Also:

- Avro 696 Shackleton T.4 (MR.1) [*Cockpit section, only*] **VP293.**

- Construcciones Aeronauticas (CASA) 2.111D (Heinkel He 111H-160 [*Front fuselage mock up*].

- Druine D.31 Turbulent **BAPC.154.**

- English Electric Canberra PR.7 **WH957.**

- Handley Page H.P.52 Hampden I **AE435.**

- Percival P.31C Proctor IV **NP294.**

- Supermarine 349 Spitfire F.VB [*Substantial remains*] **BL65.**

Fred at Partney, with gun and
rabbiting dogs, Della and Johnny, 1947.
(Fred and Harold Panton)

Edward and Frances Panton.
(Fred and Harold Panton)

Harold and gun dog Johnny,
at Old Bolingbroke, 1944.
(Fred and Harold Panton).

Evelyn in her WAAF uniform.
(Fred and Harold Panton).

Chris Panton.   *(Fred and Harold Panton).*

Binding corn at Stickford c 1953/1954, with Fred
on the binder; Bill Spinks on the tractor and standing,
Frank Hawksworth, R Clement, Edward and Frances
Panton. *(Fred and Harold Panton).*

Chris beside the tail turret of his
Halifax aircraft.
(Fred and Harold Panton).

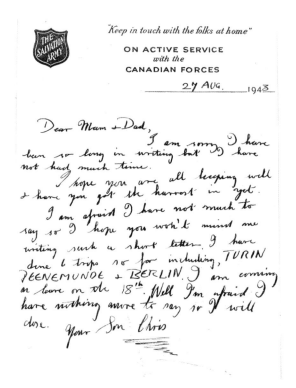

One of Chris's letters home (27 August 1943) *(Fred and Harold Panton).*

The crew of 'N' Nielsen's Nuthouse, at Topcliffe
airfield in June 1943. Left to right: Back row:
Don Awrey, Navigator; Moe McLauchlan, Rear
gunner; Harry Cooper, Wireless operator/air gunner;
Leo Milward, Bomb aimer. Front Row:
Chris Panton, Flight engineer; Chris Nielsen, Pilot.
(Fred and Harold Panton).

Cutting wheat at Stickford, 1954, with Fred on the binder;
Bill Spinks on the tractor with Fred. In the background
can be seen a timber frame barracks hut formerly part of
the RAF East Kirkby accommodation, by then being
used as a poultry house. *(Fred and Harold Panton).*

NX611 In her French Naval Air Arm colours. *(Primetime Video Productions)*

Just Jane at Squires Gate, Blackpool.
(Fred and Harold Panton).

Fred with the Burgomaster of Friessen during his first visit to Germany. *(Fred and Harold Panton).*

The site where Chris's Halifax crashed. *(Fred and Harold Panton).*

The small dance hall in Friessen, in which the surviving members of the Halifax's crew were kept overnight. *(Fred and Harold Panton).*

Chris's final resting place. *(Fred and Harold Panton).*

The main entrance to Durnbach War Cemetery. *(Fred and Harold Panton).*

NX611 arriving at East Kirkby from RAF Scampton on a 'Queen Mary' *(Primetime Video Productions).*

Squadron Leader John Willis. (1995).
This officer assisted Fred in his efforts
to purchase NX611, *Just Jane.*
(Primetime Video Productions)

RAF technicians from RAF Abingdon reassembling NX611 at East
Kirkby. *(Primetime Video Productions).*

Removing the propeller prior to the first engine being worked on.
(Primetime Video Productions).

The first engine start up. *(Primetime Video Productions).*

Fred and Harold watch pensively as the first engine is started up.
(Primetime Video Productions).

Ian in the cockpit after the second engine start-up.
(Primetime Video Productions).

Success – The brothers show their delight as the first engine
Starts. *(Primetime Video Productions).*

The East Kirkby control tower following careful restoration. *(Primetime Video Productions).*

Inside the 'Ops Room' in the restored East Kirkby control tower. *(Primetime Video Productions).*

Inside the cockpit of *Just Jane*.   The black void beyond the windscreen is reminiscent of the wartime pilots view. *(Primetime Video Productions)*.

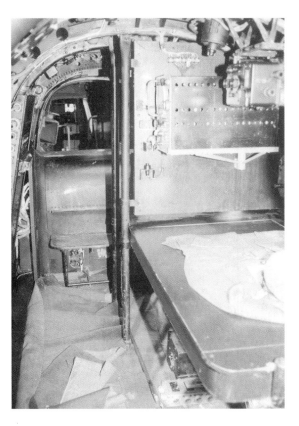

The Navigators position.
(Nigel Rutter).

The bomb Aimers position in the nose of *Just Jane*.   *(Nigel Rutter)*.

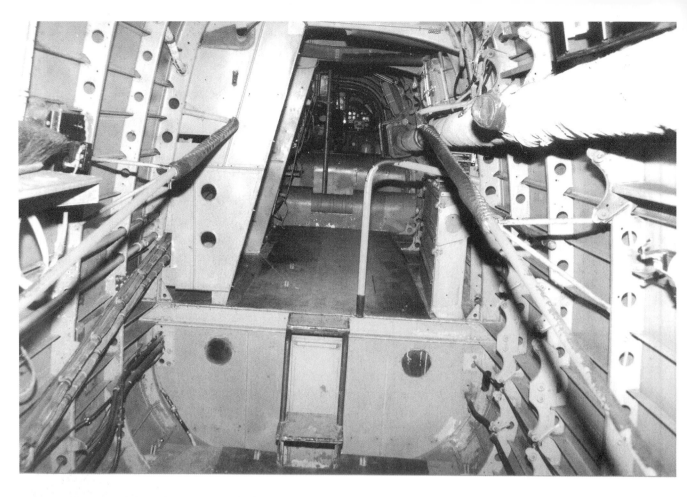

Inside the fuselage looking forward towards the cockpit. *(Primetime Video Productions)*.

The view from the cockpit roof escape hatch looking towards the tail. *(Author's collection)*

Inside the hangar – Harold and Fred with *Just Jane* and the 'bouncing bomb'. *(Primetime Video Productions).*

Cleaning and preparing *Just Jane* for the winter months. *(Primetime Video Productions).*

Mike Chatterton makes his way to the cockpit. *(Primetime Video Productions).*

The way it was………. *(Primetime Video Productions).*

617 Squadron Association members, 'Johnnie' Johnson and 'Tammy' Simpson at East Kirkby. *(Nigel Rutter).*

617 Squadron Association member, Danny Walker at East Kirkby. *(Nigel Rutter).*

Patience abounds, but still waiting some action! *(Author's collection).*

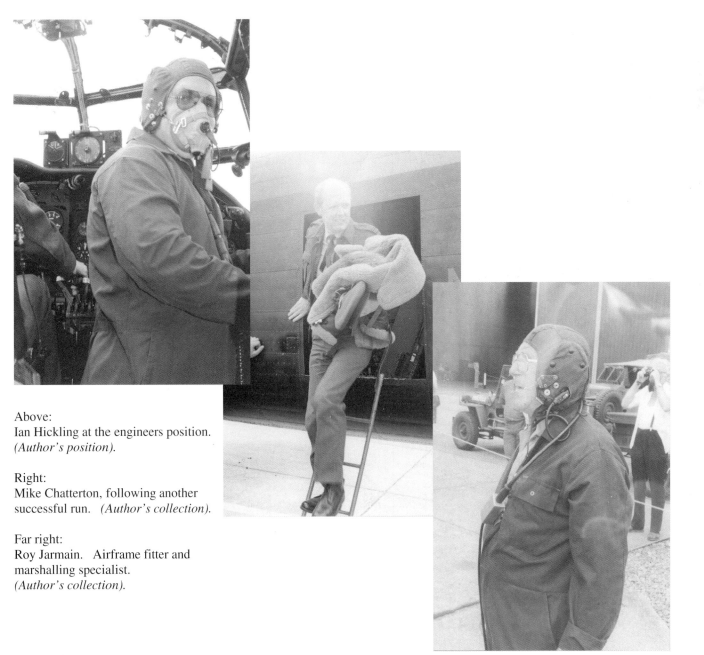

Above:
Ian Hickling at the engineers position.
(Author's position).

Right:
Mike Chatterton, following another
successful run. *(Author's collection).*

Far right:
Roy Jarmain. Airframe fitter and
marshalling specialist.
(Author's collection).

John Chatterton, ex WW11 Lancaster
pilot, and father of Mike Chatterton,
Lancaster pilot, at his home in Low Toynton.
(Author's collection).

From one Rolls Royce engine to another.
(Author's collection).

A short break during the filming of *'Two Farmers and
A Lancaster'*. *(Author's collection)*.

Fred, four in hand driving. *(Fred and Harold Panton)*.

The real *Just Jane*. Miss Cristobel Leighton Porter,
when she visited East Kirkby and met her namesake
in August 1997. *(Primetime Video Productions)*.

Just Jane is also known as *'City of Sheffield'.* *(Author's collection).*

Fred and Harold with the Lord Mayor of Sheffield, Cllr David Heslop, after the naming ceremony. *(Author's collection).*

After another busy day, *Just Jane* turns for home, to be returned to the hangar. (*Author's collection*).

Fred, Ian and Roy discuss the pros and cons of the first four engine taxi run.
(Author's collection).

All four Rolls Royce Merlins, roar out at the beginning of another taxi run.
(Author's collection).

Harry Cooper, (centre), one of the crew members who survived the crash in which
Chris Panton died. *(Primetime Video Productions).*

Just Jane, star of the BBC Television film *'Night Flight'*, which was broadcast in 2002.   With actors, technicians and the film crew in attendance.   *(Author's collection).*

Young actors fully 'kitted up' in wartime flying gear, between takes.   *(Primetime Video Productions).*

A simulated night-time German fighter-bomber attack on East Kirkby Airfield.   *(Primetime Video Productions).*

THE LINCOLNSHIRE AIRCRAFT RECOVERY GROUP

Seekers of the lost but not forgotten...

In 1973, at a time when aviation archaeology was becoming recognised as a serious and important activity, the Lincolnshire Aircraft Recovery Group (LARG) came into being. Since then, a continuous process of research and investigation throughout Lincolnshire has resulted in digs recovering many crashed aircraft or, more usually, parts of aircraft. Many of these often forgotten aeroplanes have been found along the coastline, especially the bombing ranges, where special permission had to be obtained for the group to enter.

Nowadays, regulations and controls are so strict that the work of the LARG is often restricted due to stringent safety considerations.

As an organisation, the LARG has had many 'homes' over the years, and exhibitions have been held at many fetes and air shows. Meetings used to be held at members' homes, where the cleaning of recovered parts had to be carried out in private garages. Now, however, the Group is housed in East Kirkby, at the Lincolnshire Aviation Heritage Centre, where a properly equipped workshop makes all cleaning and preparation work much easier. Members meet here on Thursday evenings at 7.30pm, and Saturday afternoons, when they work on exhibits, cleaning and preparing them for display. Photographs of digs and actual items recovered by the LARG can be seen in displays within the Heritage Centre.

Some of the Group's most notable recoveries include the Lancasters ME 625 and ME 473; Spitfire BL 655; Hampden L 4063; Vampire WZ 429; Liberators 43-95103 and P 38 Lightning 42-967211.

The LARG is a founder member of the British Aviation Archaeological Council (BAAC) and a member of the British Aviation Preservation Society (BAPC), actively supporting the aims and ideals of these organisations. Any information from the general public that will help its research is always welcomed.

As a purely voluntary organisation, funding for its various projects is dependent on subscriptions, donations and fund-raising activities by members, themselves. Membership is open to anyone over the age of 18, and a quarterly newsletter is produced to keep everyone updated on the Group's projects and undertakings.

MORE ABOUT THE AVRO LANCASTER

The concept of heavy bombers came about during the First World War, but it was not until the 1930's that really new designs were introduced, among these were the Handley Page Hampden, the Armstrong Whitworth Whitley and most successful of all the pre war designs, the Barnes-Wallis-designed Vickers Wellington. Following the outbreak of World War Two, the Whitley and the Hampden were soon found to have serious shortcomings in both performance, bomb carrying capacity and the ability to defend themselves against enemy fighters. Only the Wellington lived up to expectations and did sterling service in Bomber Command until 1942.

In 1939, Avro introduced the Manchester bomber, which was underpowered and incredibly vulnerable to ant-aircraft fire. It was also prone to take-off and landing accidents, which in the first year of its active service, contributed to over twenty per cent of all Manchester losses. It was 1941 before the Manchester airframe, the basic design of which was very sound, was finally successfully modified to become a new, extremely effective four-engine bomber – the Lancaster.

The Avro Manchester bomber was powered by two Rolls Royce Vulture engines. Roy Chadwick replaced these with four Rolls Royce Merlin V-12s. The first prototype Lancaster I, Avro 683, was converted from a standard production Manchester, BT308 and tested on 9 January 1941, by Sam Brown and Bill Thorn. A second prototype, DG595, took to the air in May, and both aircraft continued to fly throughout that year.

The first production Lancaster Mk 1, L7527, left for its maiden flight on 31 October 1941, powered by four Merlin XX engines each delivering 1,390 horsepower at takeoff. It was 69 feet long, had a wingspan of 102 feet and designed to carry fourteen 1,000lb bombs. By the end of the following month, a further three production Lancasters had were ready for flight.

Subsequent trials resulted in even further improvements to the prototype Lancasters, removing various problems as they occurred. Although the controls were relatively heavy, they could be handled as confidently as those of a fighter aircraft. The Lancaster was capable, in a steep dive, of achieving over 400mph. A Lancaster had 2,000 hp more than the Manchester and was by far the best of the three contemporary four-engine bombers in RAF service. The Lancaster had a speed, rate of climb and service ceiling that no other aircraft of that time could match. In the hands of an experienced pilot, the Lancaster also proved to be extremely effective at shaking off attacks by German nightfighters.

Weighing 36,500lbs when empty, it could take off carrying an additional 33,100lbs of fuel and bombs – almost its own weight again. Its actual fuel capacity was 2,154 Imperial gallons. It was able to carry a heavy bomb load over very long distances. Initially designed to carry fourteen 1,000lb bombs, its airframe was strengthened, and up-rated engines installed, eventually making it capable of carrying a single 22,000 lb bomb. For this purpose, special modifications involving removal of the nose, dorsal and ventral gun turrets, and the bomb doors being replaced by a streamlined fairing, eventually enabled the Lancaster to carry a single 22,000lb (Grand Slam) bomb – designed to penetrate and explode beneath the surface of concrete, creating an earthquake effect underground, such as the 'bouncing bomb' used in the raid on the Ruhr Dams did under water.

At the time of its introduction into squadron service, the Lancaster was capable of carrying out attacks against any target, at any time. They were first sent to No 44 Squadron at RAF Waddington in Lincolnshire in December 1941, followed by others going to No 97 Squadron at RAF Coningsby, also in Lincolnshire, a month later. Two of the aircraft went on the first bombing operation on 10 March 1942. Then, on 20 March 97 Squadron flew its first successful sortie. However, one crashed mysteriously at Boston, in Lincolnshire. All Lancasters were grounded for inspection, and severe testing took place – at one point killing five crewmen taking part in dummy runs. It was discovered that the structural defect in all the aircraft was due to pulled rivets along the front spar of the upper wing surfaces.

Eventually all 5 Group was equipped with the now safely modified Lancaster and, by March 1945, fifty-six Bomber Command squadrons were flying this now very successful heavy bomber.

The aircraft's first big operation, apart from mine laying, was on 17 April 1942, when both squadrons flew 1,000 miles on a raid on the M.A.N. diesel engine factory at Augsburg in Southern Germany. Led by twenty-four year-old Squadron Leader, John Nettleton, a South African, the twelve aircraft set out in groups of three on a low-level flight. One section was spotted by some Me BF109 fighters who shot down two of the Lancasters and caused another to crash-land. Fortunately, on that occasion, there was no loss of life.

Production orders for the aircraft were so great that the A V Roe Company could not cope with the numbers required, so other companies and sub-contractors, assisted in the effort to meet the Air Ministry's needs. The aircraft consisted of 55,000 separate parts and involved half a million different manufacturing operations to produce one Lancaster. Peak production occurred in August 1944 when 293 were built.

The Lancaster was not the only aircraft using Merlin engines so, before long, demand exceeded supply. The alternative engines used were the Bristol Hercules VI 14-cylinder air-cooled sleeve-valve radial engine, just as powerful and also in mass production. Known as the B Mk II, the new type of Lancaster aircraft began operations on 11/12 January 1943. Unfortunately, its maximum cruising height was well below the normal Lancaster, being only 15,000ft when fully loaded. Conversely, the air-cooled engines were less vulnerable than the

Merlins to anti-aircraft fire. The American company, Packard, undertook mass production of Merlins to ease the supply situation. Lancasters powered by the Pacard Merlin engines were designated the Lancaster B Mk III.

Another Lancaster, similar to the Mk III was produced in Canada by Victory Aircraft Ltd, also using Packard-built Merlin engines. Known as the B Mk X version, these were operated by the Canadian Squadrons of 6 Group Bomber Command, based in Britain. Yet another adaptation of the Lancaster followed – the B Mk VII, which was basically a Mk I with a couple of 0.5 inch guns in a Martin mid-upper turret mounted nearer to the wing, plus two more set in the Frazer Nash rear turret. After VJ-Day, and the installation of equipment suitable for use by Tiger Force in the tropics, they became the B Mk VII (FE).

****

Even when the war was over, Lancaster aircraft continued to play their part. A large 'pocket' in Western Holland was still in German hands and its population was nearing starvation. Many elderly and sick people had already died. After a truce had been arranged with the local German commander, Lancasters of Numbers 1, 3 and 8 Groups started to drop food supplies and clothing for the Dutch civilians in Operation Manna. Pathfinder Mosquitos 'marked' the dropping zones. One hundred and twenty-four Mosquito and 2,835 Lancaster flights were made before the Germans surrendered, the subsequent cessation of hostilities then enabling ships and road transport to enter the area. Bomber Command delivered 6,672 tons of food during Operation Manna.

Lancaster aircraft also brought troops of the British Eighth Army back from the Middle East, and they carried released prisoners of war home from all over Europe.

There is no aircraft that holds the hearts of the British people in quite the same way that the Avro Lancaster does. Its clever and awe-inspiringly beautiful design gave Bomber Command the power to play a hugely important role in winning the Second World War. Its crews undertook some of the most important and dangerous missions of those times.

Once, the night air trembled to the roar of hundreds of powerful Rolls Royce engines as numerous squadrons left Britain in these amazing aircraft on their bombing sorties. Today, if you are lucky, you will be in the right place at the right time – here at East Kirkby – to witness the maximum of eight Merlins as they roar in graceful harmony – those of the Aviation Centre's own *City of Sheffield* as she rolls purposefully along the short piece of airstrip at her disposal, still a prisoner to the ground, whilst the *'City of Lincoln'* proudly flies in acknowledgement overhead.

THE LANCASTER CREW

The Avro Lancaster carried a crew of seven – Pilot, Navigator, Flight Engineer, Wireless Operator, Mid-upper Gunner, Rear Gunner and Bomb Aimer/Front Gunner. As there was only one pilot, a built-in automatic pilot, colloquially referred to by the crews as 'George', was also installed.

Comfort was the last consideration for these young men. Once aboard their aircraft, they worked in cramped conditions and, at times, bore temperatures that fell to well below freezing. Should an aircraft be unlucky enough to be fatally hit, it also proved to be a difficult place from which to escape - with only two parachute exits: one in the floor of the Bomb Aimer's compartment in the nose, and the other the main fuselage door. The latter was a risky option, because of the possibility of striking the tail; there were also hatches in the roof. But, although described as 'ditching exits', they were all so small escaping safely was extremely difficult for someone wearing full flying kit.

Consequently, fewer than ten per cent of all aircrew survived the destruction of their aircraft.

The pilot, who was usually the aircraft's captain, sat on the left-hand side of the cockpit. He had a wide vista and was the only crewmember to have any kind of protection – a single sheet of armour plate fitted at his back. The only person further forward than the pilot was the Bomb Aimer, in the nose of the aircraft. He delivered an account of landmarks to the navigator (an operation which necessitated him lying on his stomach on the cushion at the bottom of his compartment), manned the nose turret guns when necessary, and managed the deployment of 'Window' with assistance from the flight engineer. After bomb release, a camera took photographs of the site bombed.

Immediately behind and to the right of the pilot was the flight engineer who looked after the engines and systems, managed the fuel, and tried to carry out any repairs that might be needed whilst in flight. He would also assist the pilot with throttle and pitch controls, flaps, undercarriage and – if there was an emergency – with propeller feathering and the engine fire extinguishers. At such times, he would sit upon a fold-down seat beside the pilot. Should the pilot be injured, he would usually have had enough flight instruction, to enable him to take over the controls in order to keep the aircraft on a level course.

Sat sideways at a small plotting table positioned further back inside the aircraft, the navigator kept the flight log, took frequent fixes, and gave adjustments of course and speed to the pilot. To do this, his area had to be lit, so it was curtained off. Just behind him, in line with the wing's leading edge, the wireless operator sat facing a wall of radio sets and their related equipment. Although radio silence was maintained during a mission, the radio operator had to monitor his Group frequency and listen out for any enemy radio traffic; he also operated the radio and radar jamming equipment and tail warning radar, if fitted.

The most isolated members of the whole crew were the gunners, in their cold –sometimes-icy – turrets. They looked out into the night sky where, ideally, there would be nothing for them to see. But if there was, it would be their vigilance, speed of reaction and marksmanship, upon which the rest of the crew would depend for their lives.

BOMBER COMMAND

Formed in 1936, Bomber Command was mainly employed in a passive role during the first year of World War II, the bulk of its missions being to deliver leaflets over German cities and towns. However, in the autumn of 1940 it was able to begin its intended role - attacking German industry.

It was through costly experience that Bomber Command learned that night-time sorties were infinitely preferable to those attempted in daylight, when attacks were frequently broken up by the German fighter defences and aircraft shot down almost at will. At the beginning of the night bombing campaign, there were no adequate navigational or radar aids, so crews usually had to spend a great deal of time in the air above enemy territory trying to identify intended targets. Very often they were completely unsuccessful. Fortunately, their losses due to enemy action were also very few as the German defences against night attacks were still at an elementary stage.

Comprised of five operational groups, Bomber Command was still struggling to overcome functional difficulties by the end of the first year of conflict. Its first really heavy bombers were introduced in the winter of 1940/41, but delays in their production as well as technical problems constantly enforced their withdrawal from operations. This meant that the Wellingtons and the outdated Hampdens, Whitleys and Blenheims had to be used for most of the sorties throughout 1941.

The new heavy bombers were the Short Stirling that initially went to 7 Squadron at RAF Leeming, Yorkshire in late 1940, eventually beginning operations from the 3 Group grass airfield at RAF Oakington, Cambridgeshire, in February 1941. Also first operating at the same time was the twin-engined Avro Manchester that had gone to 5 Group's 207 Squadron in late 1940. However, the Manchester had too many technical problems, mainly with its Rolls-Royce Vulture engines, so, by mid-1942, it was withdrawn from service. Next to appear was the Handley Page Halifax, used by 4 Group's No 35 Squadron and first becoming operational a month later than the previously introduced heavy bomber types.

Until July, that same year, surveys based on crew reports and night photographs showed that the success rates of night-time raids were extremely poor, sometimes even as low as only one in ten bombs landing within five miles of the aiming point. Then, the development of radar aids to navigation eased what had hitherto appeared to be a hopeless situation. Additionally, bombs were being made larger and more effective.

******

Prior to January 1942, Bomber Command had been led by Sir Richard Pierse. His successor, Air Chief Marshal A T Harris who had commanded 5 Group and held the position of Deputy Chief of Air Staff at the Air Ministry, remained Commander in Chief until the end of the war. It was his belief that strategic bombing would be the surest method of crippling Germany industry and greatly decreasing its population's morale.

The Pathfinder Force (PFF) was formed the year Harris took command. It was a Force designed to take advantage of the newly available radar devices.

At first, PFF comprised five squadrons, one from each of Bomber Command's operational groups, but by April 1945 nineteen squadrons were involved. All PFF crews were specially selected from volunteers who had a minimum of thirty operational sorties to their credit.

By the end of February 1943, the four-engined heavy bombers made up two-thirds of the force, thus increasing bomb carrying capacity by almost seventy per cent. Bomber Command was at maximum strength on 1 October 1944 when the numbers of personnel in all ranks amounted to 266,742.

Commonwealth and Allied squadrons had played their part in the air battle since 1940/41, and then in January 1943 the few RCAF squadrons that existed were combined to form 6 (RACF) Bomber Group, mainly based in Yorkshire. This group eventually expanded into fourteen heavy bomber squadrons flying Lancasters and Halifaxes, its costs being met by the Canadian Government.

By this time, scientists who were continually working on new ways of helping Bomber Command crews had come up with a number of defensive measures. These included:

♦ *'Window'* – metallised strips dropped from the aircraft whilst flying over enemy territory. They gave the same kind of signals to enemy radar as did aircraft, thus flooding control screens with both real and false readings.

♦ *'Monica'* - radar set facing rearwards that gave out a warning of enemy fighters coming up behind the bomber.

♦ *'Mandrel'* - jammed the enemy's early warning system.

♦ *'Boozer'* – a receiver that lit a warning lamp when the bomber was 'illuminated' by enemy radar transmitters. When this happened, the pilot changed course until the warning lamp went out.

♦ *'Tinsel'* – jammed the enemy's ground-to-air telephone frequencies.

A new, special group – No 100 – was formed in November 1943 exclusively to make use of these counter-measures to confuse the enemy's nighttime defences. This group eventually grew to contain thirteen squadrons.

Thanks to the Allies having gained air superiority, Bomber Command had begun regular daytime operations by 1944, over Germany and France.

For the whole of its existence during the Second World War, Bomber Command – although it may not have had an auspicious start – successfully overcame numerous obstacles, including sinking enemy vessels, sea-mining, breaching sea walls, tactical bomb dropping in support of allied ground troops, dam busting, dropping supplies, and aiding Resistance movements in enemy-occupied areas.

******

As the end of the war drew near, Bomber Command took on another role – that of saviour to the oppressed in Europe. Bomb bays were emptied of the means of death and destruction. Instead, more than three hundred Lancasters, along with one hundred and forty-five Mosquitos, carried food and clothing in Operation Manna. This took place in 1945 between 29 April and 8 May, when 6,685 tons of supplies were dropped to the starving Dutch people in Western Holland. Also, once the Germans had conceded defeat, most prisoners of war held by them were flown back to Britain by Bomber Command aircraft.

******

Bomber Command aircraft flew 392,137 operational sorties. During the bomber offensive against Germany, the Command suffered the following casualties:

♦ 56,609 killed

♦ 2,977 missing

♦ 9,890 prisoners of war

♦ 9,162 wounded

Almost one million tons of bombs were dropped by Bomber Command – 625,000 of which landed on German soil. Most of the remainder was targeted at the war at sea. As a comparison, it should be noted that the tonnage of bombs dropped on Britain by the Germans was approximately 72,000 tons.

• Between 1939 and 1945, the number of airfields built, suitable for RAF and USAAF bombers, was 430 – the total area of concrete being some 36,000 acres. The cost was £570 million.

• Wing Commander H.M.A. Day, GC, DSO, OBE, Commanding Officer of 57 Squadron at the outbreak of WWII, was shot down and taken prisoner on the Squadron's first operation, on 13 October, 1939. He escaped – and was recaptured - nine times. At other times, he was instrumental in aiding others to escape including, at the end of the war, a number of important captives of the

SS and Gestapo. For these heroic acts, he was awarded the OBE and DSO. He had already been awarded the Albert Medal for saving life some years previous; this was later converted to the George Cross. *(His story can be read in 'Wings Day' by Sydney Smith.)*

- No 55 Base, Bomber Command, RAF (Formed at East Kirkby, 15 April 1944. Disbanded in November, 1945) – **Base Commanders**:

    G/Capt R.T.Taffe OBE – 15 April 1944 to 15 May 1944

    Air Cmdr H.N. Thornton MBE – 15 May, 1944 to January, 1945

    G/Capt B.A. Casey - October 1945 to November 1945

RAF Station, East Kirkby – **Station Commanders**:

    G/Capt R.T. Taafe OBE - 20 August 1943 to 30 November 1944

    G/Capt B.A. Casey – 1 December 1944 to 30 November 1945

SNIPPETS

- Lincolnshire was the principal 'home' of the Avro Lancaster bomber. Between 1941 and 1945, 7377 were built, over fifty per cent of which operated from this county.

- Bomber Command's 6,500 Lancasters had such a short life expectancy that only thirty-five actually managed a hundred or more sorties.

- The Lancaster holding the record for surviving the most operations – 140 in total - was from Elsham airfield. It was just over two years old by the time the war ended. Sadly, it was then scrapped – a merciless fate for an aircraft that had carried its crew safely for so long.

- Thirty-five Lancasters flew one hundred or more operations – thirty of which flew, at some time, with Lincolnshire-based squadrons.

- By the time the war had reached its peak, there were forty-six operational airfields in Lincolnshire, plus other ancillary sites. Of the forty-six main airfields, twenty-four were primarily for bombers.

- It was estimated that 30,000 acres of Lincolnshire had been utilised as airfields, housing some 80,000 RAF personnel at any one time.

- Lincolnshire - Britain's Bomber County – contained a larger number of airfields, squadrons and aircraft that any other part of the country. Subsequently, it also suffered higher losses.

- Before WWII began, Lincolnshire was home to 5 Group, and the south Midlands home for 1 Group. But when war broke out, changes were made. Bomber Command allocated the southern part of Lincolnshire, along with parts of Nottinghamshire to 5 Group, whilst the northern part of the county was reallocated to 1 Group.

- By the time the end of the war was in sight, 5 and 1 Groups had a total of 720 Lancasters between them, spread over thirty-two squadrons (eighteen of these squadrons belonged to 5 Group, alone).

- 5 Group was the first to receive the Lancaster bomber, a year before 1 Group.

- 5 Group carried out the most bombing raids, a total of 70,357 sorties. These included the very first as well as the final attack of the war. It also suffered the greatest loss – 11,990 men killed and 1,888 aircraft lost in action. 1 Group lost 8,577 airmen and 1,429 aircraft.

- A 1 Group Australian squadron, No 460, which flew from RAF Binbrook for the final two years of WWII, set numerous Bomber Command records, such as dropping the highest tonnage of bombs (24,000 tons) and flying the greatest number of Lancaster raids.

- 1 Group's 101 Squadron had the RAF's first electronic counter measures unit – special 'ABC' Lancaster bombers carrying an eighth crew member who could speak German and whose radio equipment was able to locate and jam German night fighter frequencies.

- Winston Churchill, as the country's Prime Minister, visited Lincolnshire on 7 August 1940, touring defences along the county's coastline. Photographs, now at the Imperial War Museum, record Churchill inspecting troops at North Cotes and on Immingham Dock - with Captain Lord Louis Mountbatten, whose 5th Destroyer Flotilla was based there.

- On 8 August 1940, the Duke of Kent, a serving officer in the RAF, arrived in the county to inspect coastal defences.

From an Oration by Pericles, Athenian Statesman and Military Commander
(Circa 495-425 BC)

Each one, man for man, has won imperishable praise, each has gained a glorious grave – not that sepulchre of earth wherin they lie, but the living tomb of everlasting remembrance wherein their glory is enshrined. For the whole earth is the sepulchre of heroes, monuments may rise and tablets be set to them in their own land, but on the far-off shores there is an abiding memorial that no pen or chisel has traced; it is graven, not on stone or brass, but on the living heart of humanity. Take these men as your example. Like them, remember that prosperity can only be for the free; that freedom is the sure possession of those alone who have the courage to defend it.